Grown
The Black Girls' Guide to Glowing Up

MELISSA CUMMINGS-QUARRY
& NATALIE A. CARTER

ILLUSTRATED BY DORCAS MAGBADELO

BLOOMSBURY

LONDON   OXFORD   NEW YORK   NEW DELHI   SYDNEY

BLOOMSBURY CHILDREN'S BOOKS
Bloomsbury Publishing Plc
50 Bedford Square, London, WC1B 3DP, UK
29 Earlsfort Terrace, Dublin 2

BLOOMSBURY, BLOOMSBURY CHILDREN'S BOOKS and the Diana logo are trademarks of
Bloomsbury Publishing Plc

First published in Great Britain 2021 by Bloomsbury Publishing Plc
Text copyright © Natalie A. Carter and Melissa Cummings-Quarry
Illustrations copyright © Dorcas Magbadelo, 2021

Contributor text copyright © Afua Hirsch, Alexandra Sheppard, Audrey Indome, Bolanle Tajudeen, Candice Carty-Williams, Chanté Joseph, Chelsea Kwakye, Claudine Adeyemi, Rt Hon Diane Abbott MP, Dorothy Koomson, Dr Anne-Marie Imafidon MBE, Ebinehita Iyere, Emma Dabiri, Faridah àbíké-íyímídé, Fiona Timba, Georgina Lawton, Gina Knight, Hannah Lee, Ibi Meier-Oruitemeka, Jade Bentil, Jay-Ann Lopez, Trina Charles, Jamelia Donaldson, Joan Andrea Hutchinson, Jumoke Abdullahi, Kadian, Kafayat Okanlawon, Karis Beaumont, Kasey Robinson, Kayela "LaLa Love" Damaze, Kelechi Okafor, Kym Oliver, Lillian Alfred, Liv Little, Melanie Brown, Nyome Nicholas-Williams, Phoenix Brown, Rachael Corson, Raifa Rafiq, Ruby Williams, Sara Collins, Sareeta Domingo, Shakaila Forbes-Bell, Sharmadean Reid, Sharmaine Lovegrove, Sinai Fleary, Sorayah July, Tobi Olujinmi, Vanessa Sanyauke, 2021

Natalie A. Carter, Melissa Cummings-Quarry, Dorcas Magbadelo and the contributors have asserted their rights under the Copyright, Designs and Patents Act, 1988, to be identified as Authors, Illustrator and contributors of this work.

A catalogue record for this book is available from the British Library

Interior and typesetting by Pete Clayman

ISBN: 9781526623713

2 4 6 8 10 9 7 5 3

Printed and bound in Great Britain by Bell and Bain Ltd, Glasgow

To find out more about our authors
and books visit www.bloomsbury.com
and sign up for our newsletters

Contents

Foreword

By **Melanie Brown** (she/her), one fifth of the Spice Girls

I'm so proud to be part of this book. Growing up as a mixed-race girl in Leeds in the 1970s, sometimes I really didn't know who I was or where I belonged.

My mum was white, from Yorkshire, and my dad was black, from Nevis – a tiny island in the Caribbean where I'd never been and couldn't even imagine. All my family holidays were spent at a campsite in Wales with my white aunts, uncles and cousins. It was only my dad, me and my little sister, Danielle, who were brown. Life wasn't easy for my mum and dad. If they were ever out in Leeds on a Saturday when I was a baby, my mum would push me into my dad's arms because she thought there wouldn't be any trouble if he was holding a baby. **But, I never heard my dad complain about it**. When I was chased home from school by kids calling me names, he never went to complain to the teachers. Instead, he'd take me to the park and get me running and jumping as fast and high as I could – so that I'd be the one winning all the medals on sports day.

We were the only kids on our road who didn't go to the Christmas party and Easter Egg hunt at the local working men's club. They wouldn't let my dad be a member because he was Black. When I got to be a Spice Girl, I said I was going to buy that club and let everyone in. I think it's probably the reason why **I stand up for anyone who is different** – whether they are gay, straight, trans or a victim of domestic violence.

When I was little, I wanted to be white. I wanted to fit in. But I never fitted in at school anyway. I was loud, I loved to dance, I wanted more. **I became proud of my differences** – my hair, my skin, the spicy food my boyfriend's mum (who was Jamaican) made me.

When I met the Spice Girls, I found my tribe. We were all different in the way we looked, the way we spoke and our personalities, but we all wanted the same thing – to get up there and be heard. On our first ever video shoot for 'Wannabe', the stylist wanted to straighten my hair. I refused. I wasn't going to hide who I was. I wasn't going to try and fit in. I wanted my afro out there as loud and proud as I felt. The girls all backed me up. '**We celebrate our differences**,' we told them, and we did.

Becoming famous helped me own who I was because other brown and Black girls responded to me. They cheered me on, wore their hair in afros in the playground and – like me – wore (fake) leopard skin as a badge of honour. I represented them and they represented me. Nothing makes me prouder than when a brown or Black girl comes up to me today and says, 'When I saw you on stage, I felt so proud because I saw someone like me'. **Girl Power was for all of us.**

I would have loved Natalie and Melissa's book growing up. It's a book I will give to my daughters because it answers questions about who we are, from the little things that define us – like our hair – to the big things that define us – like who we are and our place in the world. It's a book that makes us conscious and a book that makes us proud. **It's been a long time coming.** Knowledge is power, but **to know who you really are is the real power**. I'm so proud to be part of this movement for girls.

Natalie

This is a really important book. This is a big deal. This is *Grown*.

For the first time, you, a beautiful, unique, special, phenomenal, creative and intelligent Black girl, have something that is written just for you. A book to show you how to own your choices. To live your truth without fear. To lead the bold, colourful life you truly deserve. To be grown **on your own terms** without limits or apologies.

For a lot of my teenage life, I struggled to feel included in British girlhood. I never saw myself in magazines, on TV shows or on the cover of the books everyone loved. It seemed that, as a young Black girl, **nothing was created with me in mind**. At the time, I just shrugged and moved on. But now I see how sad and excluded it made me feel when I couldn't read a book at school that dealt with my experiences or my culture, or pick up a magazine with a free lipstick that would actually suit my complexion.

Being a teenager and trying to understand who you are and what you want is difficult for everyone. But I don't care what anyone says, life is harder for young Black girls. Period. It can feel like everything you do is studied under a microscope. If it's not our teachers treating us differently, it's strangers being harsher on us, or our families wanting us to grow up and act like women (but not too much) before our time. So many people have opinions on what you need to do, what you can study, when you should start working and how domesticated you are. Yet, at the same time, you are being told by everyone around you to enjoy being young because you don't have 'bills to pay' or any 'real' problems. There isn't time for you to just be a **babygirl** – to be vulnerable and just be a teenager.

There are so many expectations placed on you, but the same energy isn't applied when it comes to encouraging you to embrace what makes you amazing and set your own independent path. I know that when I was younger, I felt like I couldn't just be me. It was this pressure to act like someone I wasn't that led to me holding back, not chasing my dreams with my full energy, and it made me want to shrink myself so I could be accepted. But when I reflect on it, there was never a need for me to have held back who I really was. Every Black girl is unique and special. No one has the same natural talents or perspectives, and this is what sets you apart from everyone else. **This is your life and your story**, and you get to make the choices that are best for you. You don't need to apologise for who you are.

That said, I understand that knowing yourself, loving yourself, and making decisions for yourself decisions for yourself doesn't always come naturally. All that pressure can be too much to process on your own. Sometimes you can talk to your mum, aunty, friends or a big sister, but it isn't always easy to communicate how you feel, and sometimes we worry that those around us just won't understand. Or maybe you're embarrassed or think that others might judge you.

That's where **Grown** comes in. We've taken our stories, our memories, our wins and our Ls and put them together with all the advice we wish we had when we were finding our way as young Black girls growing up. We've also asked some other inspirational Black women who we adore to share their stories and life hacks too. But don't worry, we aren't going to tell you what to do and how to live your life – because there are no right answers. In these pages, we're just going to give you our take on the things that impacted us when we were in your shoes. The questions we wanted answers to, the situations we found ourselves in and the feelings we didn't know how to articulate at the time. My wish is that this book can be the safe space you turn to when you need inspiration or comfort. Something to remind you that whatever you're going through, you're not the only one – there are others trying to work things out in the same way you are, just as we were and still are (even at our big big age).

I want this book to be everything I wish I had when I was younger. Things are always going to be harder for you when who you are isn't seen as the norm, but this book will show you that we can create our own norms. Because as long as you know your true worth and your standards, nothing will get in the way of you achieving your dreams. And that's the very essence of **Black Girl Magic** – it's doing amazing things even when you're told it isn't possible and you don't belong.

Sure, you aren't going to get everything right on the first try (or even the second one). As a young Black girl, it can feel like you won't get a second chance, like you can't just do you without having to explain or justify your actions. Life can feel like one big flop sometimes and it hurts. Sometimes you try so hard but you make so many mistakes, and even when you do everything right you still end up back at square one. It's OK to cry and admit that things haven't worked out. **There is no shame in failure.** You tried. Before you think about everything that went wrong, remember that you actually got up and walked towards doing something to better your life. Grasp that, and plan what you are going to do next time. That's what *Grown* is about – learning from our experiences and using that knowledge to drive us forward.

This book is for all Black girls. We wrote this with you in mind – you were our inspiration from the moment we came up with the idea to the moment we typed the last word. This book is for you and you alone. **We see you and we are here for you.** As a Black girl, you are not an afterthought for us – you are the centre of every chapter in this book, just as you deserve to be.

Melissa

**To whoever is reading this right now,
this book is dedicated to you.**

This book is for Black girls everywhere.

**It's our ode to Black girlhood and a celebration
of our Black British Caribbean culture.**

Grown is so special to me. It's a culmination of everything
I have learned along the way as I transitioned from a babygirl
to a big woman.

We rarely discuss it, but you already know that as a young Black girl you are
vulnerable. In so many ways, society fails to recognise that we even exist –
and that starts when we are erased from conversations about girlhood. As
Black girls, we have this weird period where we are told that we shouldn't
get involved in 'big people's business'. We're often accused of being 'too
fast' or 'nuff', and so we don't get to experience our girlhood in a way that
is afforded to our male counterparts. We don't get the 'boys will be boys'
equivalent tagline. We have all the expectations of adulthood placed upon
us without the reward.

We are treated, characterised and judged as adults before we really get
to explore and enjoy what it means to be a young Black girl. At times, it feels
like we aren't allowed to even make mistakes. We are expected to be 'grown',
to be mature, to be respectable, to wash plate and to carry ourselves
properly well before we know who we really are let alone how we feel.

Grown is our way of reclaiming a word that has been weaponised against Black girls and used to stereotype us as sometimes being too 'too much', whilst simultaneously making us feel like we aren't enough. We're turning that word on its head and giving it positive vibes. **Grown is a mood.** It's a mindset. It's a mantra. **It's a lifestyle.** It embodies everything that makes us who we are.

I can't lie. I desperately needed **Grown** when I was growing up. I was constantly searching for something that would fill in the gaps and cater directly to my experiences as a young Black girl. Like so many of us, I felt like I was taking L after L, and if it wasn't but for the support and guidance of my friends who let me know that I was never alone, things would have been tough. When I finally got sick of waiting for other people to make a space at the table for me, in the famous last words of incredible Black women everywhere, I said, 'F*** it. I'll do it myself'.

From our very first thoughts to our final words, this book is all about you, sis. In these pages we share our stories alongside important rites of passage, valuable advice and life lessons. We want to ensure you know how to shoot your shot, and in turn how to Secure the Bag. We want to give you the skills to show up and show out while making sure you're looking on point when doing it. We will be discussing self-care, well-being, beauty and skincare tips, and providing practical advice that teaches you how to make money moves that will help secure financial independence and freedom. From **fashion** to **featurism**, we are going to have honest conversations that lay bare what it means to be a young Black girl trying to get to grown. **This is the seasoning to your sauce.** That extra sprinkling of Black Girl Magic in book form.

Grown is more than just a generic toolkit or a guide. **Grown** is a complete manifestation of all the experiences of Black women who came before us. Our mothers, grandmothers, sisters and aunties. The girlfriends that listened to me rant about boys. The aunties that lent me books where Black women were the focus. Black women on the street that told me my hair looked good or that I was beautiful. Social media influencers who let me know that whatever I was feeling or thinking was ok and totally normal. The ancestors who through sheer determination and bravery made it possible for me to be here today writing the introduction to my very first book. **Grown** is an amplification of all the beauty in our Blackness.

Just know that **Grown** was created for all Black girls. When we say Black girls, we mean everyone who identifies as such. This is '**for us, by us**' because we exist, and by virtue of us existing we deserve to be represented. We don't need to ever wait to feel seen. We don't need anyone else to make us feel recognised.

From girl to grown, *The Black Girls' Guide to Glowing Up* was written with one thing in mind, sis. You.

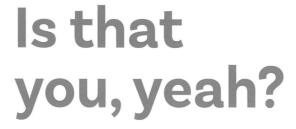

1

Is that you, yeah?

Identity and the power of self-definition

By Melissa

Growing up as a young Black girl on the outskirts of London was hard. Throw in not being able to easily see myself represented in British media, and you have a young, impressionable girl on the verge of adulthood striving to carve out an identity with little resources. There were specific issues and questions that I had, and at times it was difficult to find the right answer. Often it felt that any cultural reference to Blackness or the experiences of girls who looked and behaved like me was an afterthought, or a tick on a diversity checklist. I wanted to be catered to. **I wanted to feel seen.** I wanted to know what it was like to be a teenager. To have boy problems. To go to prom.

'I am Black, Woman, and Poet … I can choose only to be or not be, and in various combinations of myself … all that I am is of who I am, is of what I do.'
Audre Lorde [1]

I've always loved reading, so when I wanted to explore the person I was becoming, I turned to books to give me the answers I was looking for. I used to live out my rebel fantasies safely from the comfort of my own room, revelling in whatever the lead character got up to, but knowing that I wouldn't dare do the same in real life.

I was constantly seeking books that would give me that **lightbulb moment**. Something that would allow me to really make sense of the world. Someone I could identify with. Books recommended to me by friends or teachers didn't inspire me as they did them. I just couldn't relate – whether it was the food the characters ate, the things they were doing or the way they spoke to their parents, it was unfamiliar and unknown territory. **It was like being a single gungo pea in a bowl of rice.**

Of course, I could still find joy in reading stories written about people with different experiences, but I also became more conscious of my lived differences. I remember reading *Pride and Prejudice* by Jane Austen and falling in love with the character, Elizabeth Bennet. She was smart, gutsy, bold and witty – everything I hoped and dreamt I could be. I saw myself in her and imagined finding my own Mr Darcy, but it always felt bittersweet finishing the book. **Something was missing.** But I hadn't yet learnt the words I needed to vocalise the frustrations I felt.

It wasn't until I turned fourteen and read *Their Eyes Were Watching God* by Zora Neale Hurston that I finally felt seen. Hurston introduced me to the concepts of feminism before I knew them by name. I was thrilled to read a book written in a dialect reminiscent of the patois spoken in my own home. To witness a Black protagonist explore her womanhood, sexuality and independence was mind-blowing. Hurston showed me the importance of financial freedom, the beauty of love and friendship, the power of setting boundaries and speaking your mind. Although the book was written during the Harlem Renaissance of the 1920s and 30s, I felt more connected to Janie, the protagonist, than I had to a character in any other book I'd read before. For once I felt centred. **This was representation.**

'"How can anybody deny themselves the pleasure of my company? It's beyond me!" This is exactly right. No one should deny themselves the pleasure of Zora.'
Zadie Smith [2]

Hurston didn't feel the need to explain the meaning of the words she used, or the food her characters ate. I distinctly remember characters eating cornmeal dumplings, fried chicken and macaroni. It was in that moment that I truly understood the meaning of the phrase, '**What is understood, does not need to be explained**'. Those are soul food delicacies for me – that's 'yard' cooking – and they symbolise comfort and love. It's like when your mum or grandmother notices you aren't yourself, so they cook you up some dumplings or take time out to fry some chicken. **It's equal to a big hug.** Without words, those foods just manage to let you know that everything will be OK. To this day, if Natalie and I have had a tough day or we want to celebrate, the first thing we do is ensure we find a bossman so we can get some hot wings.

'If you kin see de light at daybreak, you don't keer if you die at dusk. It's so many people never seen de light at all.'
Zora Neale Hurston [3]

This is why Hurston's book is so important to me. Not only did it make me realise that our stories need to be told, it showed me that Black women deserve to be depicted in ways that are familiar and recognisable. Until then, I didn't understand just how much I needed to see parts of myself represented in literary fiction. To be more than just a plot device (or for those of you who are studying English literature, the 'magical negro').

Their Eyes Were Watching God quickly became my manifesto. I have read it so many times and at different points in my life, and the older I get, the more things I discover about the text and about myself. When I'm feeling conflicted, I reach for it, finding comfort in reading words written about a Black woman simply existing. **Through finding Hurston, I ended up finding myself.**

'Two things everybody's got tuh do fuh theyselves. They got tuh go tuh God, and they got tuh find out about livin' fuh theyselves.'
Zora Neale Hurston [4]

I guess this is one of the reasons I wanted to create a space like Black Girls Book Club that allowed Black women to express themselves unapologetically. Using our love of books as a link of commonality and a way to grow our **sisterhood**. Natalie and I wanted to ensure that there was a platform where Black women were celebrated, centred and catered to. We understood that we needed a space to explore what Professor Kimberlé Crenshaw meant when, in 1989, she defined the term '**intersectionality**'.

'Consider an analogy to traffic in an intersection, coming and going in all four directions. Discrimination, like traffic through an intersection, may flow in one direction, and it may flow in another.'

Professor Kimberlé Crenshaw [5]

Put simply, when you understand what it means to be the person standing in the middle of an intersection of oncoming traffic – knowing that at any moment danger could strike from one direction because of your gender, or the other because of your race – you ultimately understand what it means to be Black and a woman. This is intersectionality.

Black Girls' Book Club sits at that intersection. But we've reclaimed that space, making it special, sacred and safe – a place where Black women's rich and varied experiences and complex identities are our strengths, not our weaknesses. This space allows us to define ourselves and reject damaging cultural stereotypes such as the 'angry, loud Black girl', 'strong Black woman' or 'sassy girlfriend'. It gives us the opportunity to discuss our unique experiences and unpack what it actually means to be Black, a woman, and all the other elements that together make up our individual identities. If through Hurston I found myself, through Black Girls' Book Club I truly began to understand who I was becoming.

I want you to see this chapter as an opportunity to take stock and think about who you are. A space to allow you to look back at yourself and embrace every element of what makes you *you*. Remember, neither you nor I should be bound to the expectations of others – you are who YOU say you are, and not what others purport you to be.

'My Blackness does not inhibit me from being beautiful and intelligent. In fact, it is the reason I am beautiful and intelligent. And you cannot stop me.'
Amandla Stenberg [6]

What is identity?

Your identity is simply who you are. It's the characteristics that make you unique. From the way that you walk and the way that you talk to the things you like to do. Your identity can be influenced by many factors, from your culture, religion and race, to your hobbies and life goals. I feel like **everything I've done up to this point has shaped me**. Every person I've met. Every book I've read. Every holiday I've been on. Every mistake I've made. All of those interactions have informed the person I am and the person I'm still becoming.

When I think about my identity, I realise that even at my big big age, I still don't have all the answers. I change my mind about things – whether it's about my personal life, my career or my boundaries – as often as I change my hair. That's not to say these things are trivial – I'm just saying that being older doesn't necessarily make you any surer of yourself.

Sometimes, I don't have the right words to articulate the way I'm feeling, or the capacity to deal with the bubbling thoughts and emotions that are coursing through my body. And that **not knowing is perfectly OK**. Do not feel obligated to stick to any decisions you make, or to have an immediate, fully formed response to the things that are happening around you. **Finding yourself often means acknowledging that nothing is static – things, thoughts and ideas are forever changing.** Who you are today may not be who you were yesterday, and definitely not the person you will be in ten or twenty years.

'I'm a Black woman who is from Central Falls, Rhode Island. I'm dark-skinned. I'm quirky. I'm shy. I'm strong. I'm guarded. I'm weak at times. I'm sensual. I'm not overly sexual. I am so many things in so many ways.'
Viola Davis [7]

Identity is a work in progress

Georgina Lawton (she/her), author, speaker, freelance journalist and founder of the podcast The Secrets in Us

The formation of your identity doesn't happen in a vacuum. By that I mean, no one becomes the person they are without a little help from the structures around them. School. Family. College. The Church. The Mosque. Your dance class. The local football club. Who you are is a result of all these influences as well as various personal choices over the years. But, sometimes it may feel like others have a little too much say in who you are becoming. You may feel like you don't fit in, or that being your authentic self results in rejection or condemnation. Identity struggles are isolating and draining, but I *promise* you they are a part of growing up. Personal identity battles are universally experienced, depicted in everything from *Harry Potter* to *The Hunger Games*, from religion to rap, and from philosophy to pop and politics. Humans have concerned themselves with the search for self for thousands of years. For Black girls, our journey is often tougher, taking place against a global landscape that often fails to see our joy and pain, or hear our feelings. You may feel like a perpetual outsider, a person for whom a fully-formed identity feels like a destination that is forever beyond your reach. But know that you have the power. **The boundaries of your personhood can only be drawn by you.** A clear sense of self is a work in progress, a journey you may be on for your entire life. So, read widely. Write down your thoughts and feelings. Seek counsel in those who inspire you. And, little by little, you will learn to trust in your own decisions for yourself, so that one day, the person you see in the mirror is loved, lauded, heard and understood – not just by others – but by you too.

So, how do you define yourself?

Figuring out who you are or where you are going isn't going to be an easy task. At my big age I still feel like I'm finding things out about myself and learning who I am. I continue to transition and to grow. Constantly learning and unlearning things as I go. Meeting new people and having new experiences have helped me to define myself by my own rules. At this point it doesn't matter what clothes I wear, who I know or even what I look like. There's more to who I am than what I see when I look in the mirror. Now, honey, that doesn't mean that I won't buy the latest Fenty Skin, make-up, shoes, handbag, or whatever Bad Gal RiRi is selling. But I acknowledge that my worth isn't based on how others view me. **I'm enough.** Period.

> 'If I didn't define myself for myself, I would be crunched into other people's fantasies for me and eaten alive.'
> **Audre Lorde** [8]

So, I challenge you to create an identity mind map. Set out the things that are important to you, the things that make you tick. Start by writing down three phrases that describe you – these could be anything from your hair type to your religion to your cultural background. Next, add three things that are important to you – they could be your family, friends or a hobby. Now, think about what particular qualities you bring to the table. Are you a reliable friend or a good listener? Do you make people laugh or are you a great dancer? These are your unique strengths – add them to your mind map!

I don't bring anything to the table – I am the table!

Writing things down isn't the only way to do this. You could cut out pictures from a magazine or, if you prefer, record this exercise as a voice note to come back to when you need to centre yourself.

A mind map doesn't exactly help you to create your identity, but it allows you to visualise all the different and intersecting parts of who you are. If at any time you start to feel like you're unsure of yourself, I want you to look back at this. Remember, **you are all these things and more**. At times, when I'm not feeling myself, I like to think about the different attributes I have and the things I have achieved. It's a helpful hack I learnt to help instantly calm my nerves whenever I'm feeling anxious, or when I need the courage and motivation to complete a task.

I acknowledge this is all very easy to say, but tough to actually do. Sometimes, you may feel as though your worth is about who you are friends with or the trainers you wear. **I totally get it.** I remember that having a pair of Kickers or a Baby G watch automatically meant you were a bad gyal when I was at school. It seems so insignificant now, but turning up at school after the summer holidays to find your friends are wearing Kickers while you are wearing Clarks really hurts. And your parents just don't get it. It's as if everyone got the memo. Everyone knew exactly what to do to fit in. Except you.

Sometimes, it isn't even about material things. It might be the activities you do or what grades you get at school. This was definitely true for me. I took part in an excessive amount of after-school activities – even at a young age, it was really important for me to show how capable I was. Yes, it looked great on my personal statement and I picked up life skills that I use to this very day. But, looking back, I realise that I was using the things I could do or experiences I'd had in place of letting people see who I was as a person. There was more to me than what I did, who I knew or the clothes I liked to wear. I had to strip away all the extras and think about who I was without the good grades. The Baby G watch. Or my friends. When everything you are is wrapped up in what you can *do* and what you *like* rather than who you actually are, it can be quite life shattering when you don't meet up to your own expectations.

So, rather than worrying about how great I was doing in school, compared to everyone else, I started to think about whether I praised myself for the hard work I put in. I started celebrating how many questions I got right, rather than beating myself up for the ones I missed. **I took time to love myself for who I was rather than what I could do.** But it's hard! To this day I still have to remind myself that I deserve praise not because of what I can contribute, but just for who I am.

See and be seen

Although it's ultimately up to you to define yourself, part of your identity is also about how other people see you – and other people's viewpoints can offer a fresh perspective. Often, we are our own worst critics and we don't realise the positive ways in which we impact people's lives until they tell us.

Ask a friend to write down five phrases that describe you and do the same thing for them. When you're ready, swap your lists. I bet you'll be surprised with some of the things they've written down – they might have highlighted strengths you weren't even aware you had!

1. ....

....

....

2. ....

....

....

3. ....

....

....

4. ....

....

....

5. ....

....

....

Dig a little deeper

I feel that really knowing and embracing who you are is the first step to becoming grown. When I look in the mirror, I see myself as a Black British woman of Caribbean heritage. No matter what I experience or who I meet, that is a fact that will never change. **I'm proud of my culture**, and I love the way it influences and informs the person I am and the decisions I make – whether that's placing a capful of Dettol in my bath, making life-changing decisions based on whether 'my spirit takes to it', or spending a whole year planning my outfit for the single most important date in my calendar. (No, not my birthday – Notting Hill Carnival!) It's there when I hear lovers rock or reggae music being played in the early hours of the morning, and instinctively know that my weekend plans are ruined because my mum wants us to clean the house from top to bottom. It's there when I'm using my mouth to point at things, and when Natalie starts saying, 'Hello, hello, hi!' when someone is doing something wrong and they need to stop IMMEDIATELY.

My particular cultural background means understanding that the act of kissing your teeth can have 100 different meanings. It's deciphering exactly which 'ting' my Dad wants me to get. ('No, it's not dat ting. It's the other ting next to the big ting.') It's eating fried dumplings, baked beans and having a cup of Yorkshire Tea. Or a roast dinner with rice and peas, macaroni pie and some Guinness punch. It's repeating a word or phrase twice for emphasis (describing something as 'good up, good up' definitely holds more weight than simply saying it was 'good'). Understanding where these parts of my character come from only helps to understand the person I am.

Now, you may have read my experiences above and not necessarily seen parts of your own culture captured. It is important to remember that we all access our different cultures in different ways. For many of us who are first, second and third-generation immigrants, the preparation and serving of traditional dishes is a simple way of **celebrating our heritage**. For me, nothing beats a Julie mango, sugar cane or a plate of my mum's curry goat. But for you, it may be about using a familiar language at home, reciting Anansi stories, dressing up in aso ebi for a special occasion, doing a particular dance or taking part in customs such as Nine Night. It could be tied up in the way you practise religion, or you might access it by listening to family members reminisce about their lives back home.

One of my favourite things to do is to listen to my grandma regale me with stories about growing up in Jamaica. These stories help me feel closer to her and allow us to connect with one another despite our generational differences. This not only helps to demystify my culture, it also allows me the space to embrace or reject parts of my upbringing with true knowledge and understanding of where it comes from. She also tells me honestly about the racism she faced when she emigrated to the UK, and the different ways she supported other people in her community to adapt to life here. She talks of the importance of performing libations when someone passes away, and describes the parties she attended and the number of suitors she had. This is a history masterclass, a way of passing stories and knowledge down from grandmother to granddaughter like a griot, and it forms part of our tradition. Having this cultural connection has empowered me to be confident in who I am and where I've come from.

Generational stories

Jade Bentil, feminist historian and author

The first time I sat down to interview my grandma about her memories of arriving in Britain from Ghana in the late 1950s, I didn't know quite what to expect. A gifted storyteller, I knew that for the next few hours she would transport me back in time. I expected to relive the journey with her, listening to her recollections of the moment she'd purchased a one-way boat ticket to Liverpool, or the moment she'd finally arrived after twelve days at sea, shocked by just how cold and how dark this place called England was. What I didn't know when I started to record our conversations is just how much they would change my life.

My grandma has lived a life that would be impossible to narrate here in all its splendour. I learnt so much about her: her hopes and her dreams. The way she has loved and has been loved. These conversations lay the groundwork for my forthcoming book, *Rebel Citizen*. Alongside my grandma, I've interviewed nearly thirty women across the country about their memories of arriving in Britain following the Second World War. These women were the original Hot Girls—women who challenged the climate of racism, sexism and classism in Britain to live the full, beautiful lives that they imagined for themselves. I hope that in recording their stories, I can contribute documenting the incredible lives that our foremothers have created and passed down to us.

So, how do you learn about your culture when you are the second or even third generation to be born in this country? Your family might have been here long before Windrush. You may be of mixed heritage, meaning that navigating your cultural background might be more difficult, especially if you're not in regular contact with family members who share your history. You may have a close connection to your relatives, but don't feel comfortable asking them personal questions about their lives.

No matter the situation, there is always a way to learn more. You may wish to travel and explore your cultural home. Perhaps written histories and old photographs are your thing – the Black Cultural Archives in Brixton, London is a really good place to start. For those of you who want to explore your culture through food, the Latin Village in Seven Sisters, Tottenham is filled with shops and cafés where you can get plátanos maduros, empanadas and arepas. One of my favourite things to do is watch Nollywood films with my BFFs. It's so affirming to see women who look like me on screen, and it also gives me an opportunity to connect with my friends through their own culture. Don't forget your community centre – for many of our parents, coming to the UK meant learning a new set of rules, navigating British bureaucracy and even figuring out the best place to purchase things like plantain and shea butter. Your local community centre is a really good place to start learning about your culture and identity.

And whilst Notting Hill Carnival is Europe's biggest street festival, Birmingham, Derby, Huddersfield, Leeds and Luton do an incredible job of uplifting and celebrating Caribbean culture through playing mas. Somali Week Festival was founded by Ayan Mahamoud MBE as a response to the lack of provisions for Somali arts and culture in the UK. She created her organisation 'Kayd' – meaning 'preservation' in Somali –

as a way of protecting and promoting Somali arts, culture and heritage.

You can also connect with like-minded people through social media by following Instagram accounts that you can relate to. I really recommend reading books by authors who have a similar background to you – whether that's Nicole Dennis-Benn, Chimamanda Ngozi Adiche, Alexandra Sheppard or Camryn Garrett. Choose whatever option works for you!

'Third culture kid'

Sareeta Domingo (she/her), editor and author

For a long time growing up, I felt jealous of people whose identity was shaped by where they were from. My parents are from Sierra Leone, and I was born in south-east London. However, my family moved house a lot. We lived in Kent and East Sussex, in areas where there were almost no other Black families. Then, my mum and dad told me and my twin brother that we were moving again for my dad's job – but this time all the way to Bahrain, in the Middle East. My silly, nine-year-old brain definitely pictured us riding to school on a camel, but I was hyped for that!

Growing up in Bahrain until I was sixteen was an amazing experience. We had a wonderful lifestyle, incredible education, and my friends were literally from all over the world. However, there were hardly any other Black kids there either, and when I came back to the UK I still felt a sense of rootlessness when it came to my identity. I'd grown up without friends who had a shared cultural heritage, so it was harder for me to understand who I was. I later heard the phrase 'third culture kid', meaning someone raised in a culture other than their parents' or the culture of their country of nationality, and who also live in a different environment for a big part of their childhood. That's me! I worried that it would be hard for me to find 'my people', or that I'd be judged as strange for not being the 'same' as other young Black British women.

However, there is no *one way* to be Black. Forging connections with people is about so much more than just knowing where you are from. I have a wealth of experiences that have shaped my identity, and, no matter where I go now, I know that I'm a proud Black British woman of Sierra Leonean heritage.

What being Jamaican means to me and my work

Sara Collins (she/her), award-winning author

I left Jamaica when I was four years old, and sometimes it feels as if I've spent every day since then trying to return. I moved to Grand Cayman, and later came to school in England. When you leave your birthplace as a very young child it slips away from you; you can feel as if you are spending your whole life trying to catch it. I think this is why I was drawn to reading. It is also why I write. It's my way of claiming territory for myself, of finally putting down some roots.

What does being Jamaican bring to my work? In a word, everything. I believe that our status as islanders sets us up to be observers of the world: it's in our DNA. We are a diasporic nation, so we are curious, and connected. We travel. We know about transitions, and about yearning. We know about interrogating ideas of home, and belonging. We know about making one people out of many, and something out of nothing, about honouring history while at the same time shaking off its chains. I will probably always write about Jamaica in some way, even if doing so will never quite bring me home.

Documenting our history

Karis Beaumont, photographer and founder and curator of Bumpkin Files, a multimedia platform centred around Black life in Britain

I document the Black British experience because all Black history is important. Throughout the years, our histories have been left out, whitewashed or erased. When we look at Black British culture, we're rarely celebrated, especially from outside of London. As a photographer, I believe it's my duty to ensure that our stories and experiences are included, preserved and told. Black British girlhood is so unique. We all come from different cultures, walks of life and are pretty badass if I'm being honest!

On being an Efik woman

Lillian Alfred (Effiong) (she/her), law graduate, mentor for a social mobility charity and relationship associate in corporate and investment banking

'Efik? What's that? In Nigeria? Abeg. I just class you all as Igbo. It's easier'. This is a common response to whenever I tell people my ethnic origin. At times I laugh, but there are times when I am completely exasperated. Often the dismissive comments are never ill intentioned, but it's nice when someone just GETS it, or is open to learning about my culture without weird generalisations or stereotypes.

'What's the big deal? Are you not just Nigerian?' people ask. Well, actually the three most populous ethnicities or languages in Nigeria are Yoruba, Igbo and Hausa. However, did you know that in Nigeria that there are more than 250 ethnicities and over 500 languages spoken? Maybe not. Efik is one of those languages. Despite Nigeria being the most populous Black country in the world, I am of Efik descent – which is a minority group. Nigeria is a man-made country that has a variety of cultures and ethnicities. Thus, not only am I a minority as a Black British Woman born and raised in London but I am also a minority as a woman of Efik descent from Nigeria.

Nevertheless, if you ever meet an Efik person, you would come to realise that the term 'minority' is not something we would use to describe ourselves. We are very proud people with rich culture and traditions – all of which has made me the person I am today. We have twenty-seven national food dishes and, like many cultures, we are incredibly passionate about music and dance. I have fond memories of rehearsing a dance from primary school to a pop song and my mother telling me, 'Don't dance with just your hands and legs. Soften your back for goodness sake'. I love our traditional attire, such as Oyonyo, as well as what takes place for marriage rites. I love how women are revered in our culture and have a strong sense of self. I believe those values, as well as many others, have set me in good stead to steer my way through life, and are what has helped me my own personal Black British journey as an Efik woman.

Identity is a work in progress

Ebinehita Iyere (she/her), founder of
Milk & Honey, a platform that centres Black
British girls

I don't know what my experience should or shouldn't have been as a Black British girl because it's never been documented. I was rushed into becoming a Black woman by society.

Black British girlhood is not a linear path, but a navigation of individual and shared, emotional and physical connections and experiences. Whilst our unique aesthetic, culture and style defines our girlhood, it is important to remember that peace within and self-care is just as important as our outward presentations. Claiming a stake in your identity as a Black British girl creates a pathway for you to be free to be creative and credited; fragile without judgment; and to discard the stereotypes that our self-expression is nothing but rage or that you have to be strong whilst being able to bend for the comfort of others.

Many Black women did not get a chance to be Black girls. One could argue that this was a method of survival – a coping mechanism to give a Black girl a fighting chance in a world where we are not seen, let alone heard. That's why, through Milk & Honey, I work to centre our experiences and celebrate our accomplishments. I want to ensure visibility for all Black girls and provide them with safe spaces to discuss their achievements and challenges, and support them to achieve their hopes and dreams.

Never forget that you are the embodiment of all of your experiences, and you are exceptional.

Finding myself

Sharmaine Lovegrove (she/her), publisher at Dialogue Books

I truly believe that being your full self is the best gift you can bring to the world. We all make mistakes, and all have flaws, but learning from the past and not defining yourself by your imperfections is important to create a peaceful, full life where you can fulfil your potential.

I epitomised a care-free Black girl when I was a teenager in South London in the 1990s. I loved grunge music as much as I love curry goat, I wore my hair natural and rocked Dr. Martens boots, Nirvana T-shirts and patchwork skirts. My personal taste was an expression of my youth and liberalism, but was oppositional to the quiet, conservative, Jamaican family I am from. It was important to me to show that I could be a loving, studious grandchild with an interest in Marxism and heavy basslines.

As I walked through Brixton to my home in Battersea, I would be called 'coconut' by random young people on road, but I would retort by quoting the righteousness of Blackness from Dr Martin Luther King, James Baldwin or Malcom X. I stood firm in who I was and walked with pride and was able to rise above the criticism, empowered by the knowledge I was gaining and fun in the experiences I was have having.

Self-knowledge is power and it builds resilience and confidence, which are important attributes to have when navigating the modern world. There are many challenges we have to face in the world, but don't let one of those battles be with your true self.

On race, gender and disability

Jumoke Abdullahi (she/her) and **Kym Oliver**
(she/them), creators of the Triple Cripples, an
activist platform that centres people of colour
living with disabilities

We understand what it means to go through life as Black, Disabled women. Simply put, the world was not created, nor structured with us in mind. Society has already decided what we deserve and, unfortunately, the answer is, not much. We get what it feels like to look around and not see yourself reflected anywhere. This can be an incredibly isolating experience. That's why we created the Triple Cripples platform and community – to cater specifically to you. To centre and speak directly to your needs, hopes, fears and desires. So, here is what we would like you to do: Be **BIG**.

Take up space. We will make room for you. Space has already been made for you. So often we are reduced to horrifying statistics, either because of our Blackness or our disabilities and/or chronic illnesses. The often negative social, cultural, financial and medical implications of our lives are discussed in news articles and within the political arena. However, they sorely lack the range to appreciate the nuances that exist at the intersections of race, gender and ability. While there is much that needs to be fixed, unlearned and redesigned about the structure of the world. There is a lot of joy, laughter and love to be found in our lives. We just want you to know that we see you, hear you and love you. We are you.

Self-image

It's so easy to get into the habit of comparing yourself to others. Especially when it's so easy to go onto social media and within seconds see twenty different people living an enviable lifestyle, getting hundreds of thousands of likes for simply standing there and taking a picture in their room. Whether it's someone with better grades than you, nicer clothes, more friends, someone thinner than you or thicker than you – there's always going to be someone out there that seemingly has the most perfect life and everything you want.

'When I'm not feeling my best, I ask myself, "What are you gonna do about it?" I use the negativity to fuel the transformation into a better me.'
Beyoncé [10]

Attempting to maintain a positive self-image is sometimes a lot easier said than done. It just takes one scroll to change how you feel about yourself. That's the danger of comparison culture – no matter what you do, no matter what lengths you go to or how you try to change there will always be someone who has something you don't.

So, how do you keep a **positive self-image** when there is so much pressure around you to conform? First things first. I would suggest only following and engaging with those that make you feel affirmed and good about yourself.

'[You] don't have to be like me – you need to be like you, and never ever let somebody stop you or shame you from being yourself.'
Lizzo [11]

Unfollow. Block. Delete

If it makes you feel bad, or forces you to contrast and compare, then babygirl, it's not for you. Surround yourself with images of those who look like you and make you feel on top of the world. The worst thing you can do for your mental health is to continue to expose yourself to things that make you feel less than. Once you start seeing the value in who you are, your confidence and feelings of self-worth will increase.

'Believe in yourself. Push to your highest limit. Be confident that you can do it. If you take that one push to do it, then God's got the rest. Just leave it up to him.'
Marsai Martin [12]

Half the time, confidence is all about faking it until you make it. Yeah, it's pretty cringey to keep telling yourself how great you are, but you have to be your own cheerleader. Confidence comes from knowing who you are and seeing the power in what you can do. You can be confident in your abilities and still be awkward or anxious.

I want you to try something. Look at yourself in the mirror and say these words:

'I'm destined for GREAT things. I stay READY. I'm OWNING the person I am becoming. I'm WORKING towards my goals. I will NEVER let you dull my shine. I'm GROWN. PERIOD.'

Repeat this every day for a whole week. How does it make you feel?

Understanding self-love

Kelechi Okafor (she/her), podcaster, writer and actress

It takes a brave person to experience situations that could make you believe that you are undeserving of love, yet still go outward and inward to embody that love anyway.

The first step to self-care is to remember to breathe. Sounds simple enough, yet it is a transformational practice. Sometimes, life can get overwhelming and we don't even realise that we are holding our breath. Checking in with our breathing allows us to re-centre and to be present in the particular moment.

Role models

Sometimes, thinking about who you are, what you're going through or what is expected of you can feel overwhelming. In those moments, I think about women who have inspired me. **Black women who empowered me to define who I wanted to be.** Often, I identified with them because they had a similar background to me. Sometimes, they were women who inspired me purely because they had achieved exactly what I was working towards. Having the privilege of being able to draw inspiration from Black women who came before me has always given me that extra push. They show that not every door is shut. For just a moment, the glass ceiling shatters.

'I don't know her.'
Mariah Carey [13]

For me, one of those women is Mariah Carey. Now, Ms Carey is not just the patron saint of Black Girls' Book Club, she is also my big sis (in my head). In fact, Ms Carey calling into BBC Radio and talking about BGBC was probably the most surreal moment of my life! I love everything about her, from her overuse of the word 'dahhhling' to her penchant for the highest of heels and the tightest of dresses. I also find Mariah **incredibly inspiring** – and not just because she knows the art of SHADE, honey (she did give us the iconic phrase 'I don't know her') – but because she has dominated the charts since the 1990s, basically invented the remix and was one of the first artists to take the pop/hip-hop genre we have all come to love mainstream. And she did all this by being unapologetically herself. She used her talent to take up space and create a lane for herself in a male-dominated industry, despite the odds being stacked against her. She didn't come from a wealthy family. She didn't go to uni. She didn't take music lessons and, despite her five-octave range, she can't read sheet music. But she did have talent, faith, self-belief and fearlessness. That, for me, is super inspirational. So, when I feel low, I ask myself, **'What would Mariah Carey do?'** and it helps inspire me to think outside the box and believe in myself.

So, here's a task for you. Think of five people who inspire you. They can be friends, family members or famous faces. Write a short sentence explaining what makes them so special and how they make you feel.

1. ....
2. ....
3. ....
4. ....
5. ....

If you're stuck, I've written a few of my own below. When I'm feeling down and I'm trying to make sense of the world, I search for interviews, articles and videos about my role models to help me out of that rut.

★ Filmmaker Ava DuVernay reminds me that it's never too late to start.

★ Rt Hon Diane Abbott MP teaches me the power of community.

★ Beyoncé showed me that there are endless possibilities when you have a strong work ethic.

★ STEM entrepreneur Dr Anne-Marie Imafidon MBE is the reason I know that nothing is impossible and that the sky is the limit.

★ Rapper Lil' Kim inspired me to trust my voice and be unapologetically myself.

★ Naomi Campbell has dominated the modelling industry for more than thirty years, demonstrating the importance of self-belief and honing your craft.

Take time to reflect

I understand that all this talk on identity might feel like it's all a bit much and something many of you just won't have the capacity to engage with right now. And that's OK. **Life can be complex.** And your identity is always evolving. Remember, you can come back to this chapter at any time. I got you!

For those of you who just want to listen to some music, watch a film or read a book while you figure things out, here are some suggestions that I feel portray the Black girl experience. Perhaps you will have that epiphany moment like I did when I discovered Zora Neale Hurston, or maybe exploring the artists below will inspire you to pick up your own pen and create something. Just remember that you can be all of the things we have discussed, or none of them. You might be great at sport, an academic, a thinker or maybe you're not too sure who you are or what you're good at yet. Don't worry, sis. **No matter what, your uniqueness is your secret weapon.**

'Over 90% of entertainment is produced by white men. I'm a part of a lineage of creators who want to change that narrative. You can tell when a show is made by a sister.'
Ava DuVernay [12]

TV AND FILM

Girlhood
Pose
The Proud Family
Girlfriends
Grown-ish
On My Block
Sister, Sister
Insecure
Moesha
Paris Is Burning

Rocks
Love & Basketball
Beasts of the Southern Wild
Jinn
Little
Queen of Katwe
Greenleaf
I May Destroy You
Akeelah and the Bee

Disclaimer: Some of the suggestions here may contain adult content. Always check with a parent or guardian before deciding whether to watch, read or listen.

'She didn't read books so she didn't know that she was the world and the heavens boiled down to a drop.'

Zora Neale Hurston [15]

IF YOU LIKE ... BOOKS ... TRY

Pride and Prejudice → **Keisha the Sket** by Jade LB

To Kill a Mockingbird → **The Hate U Give** by Angie Thomas

Angus, Thongs and Perfect Snogging → **Oh My Gods** by Alexandra Sheppard

Bridget Jones's Diary → **Queenie** by Candice Carty-Williams

The Story of Tracy Beaker → **The Poet X** by Elizabeth Acevedo

Little Women → **Americanah** by Chimamanda Ngozi Adichie

Harry Potter and the Philosopher's Stone → **Children of Blood and Bone** by Tomi Adeyemi

The Handmaid's Tale → **Noughts and Crosses** by Malorie Blackman

Are you there, God? It's me, Margaret → **Full Disclosure** by Camryn Garrett

To All the Boys I've Loved Before → **The Sun is Also a Star** by Nicola Yoon

MUSIC

Beyoncé - *Lemonade*
Kelis - *Kaleidoscope*
Solange - *A Seat at the Table*
Summer Walker - *Over It*
Mariah Carey - *The Emancipation of Mimi*
Lauryn Hill - *The Miseducation of Lauryn Hill*
Ari Lennox - *Shea Butter Baby*
Tiwa Savage - *R.E.D.*

'[I'm proud of] the femaleness of the album, of the freaking outspokenness of it, the Blackness of it, the alternativeness of it.'

Kelis [16]

I woke up like this

Skincare and self-love for beautiful brown-skin girls

By Natalie

'I woke up like this' isn't just an affirmation about having an effortlessly fresh and naturally beautiful face all day, every day – it is a battle cry of self-love and confidence. Yet, the hardest part of loving yourself can sometimes be loving the skin you are in.

"Be healthy and take care of yourself, but be happy with the beautiful things that make you, you.' Beyoncé [1]

We all feel pressure to have our face beat and our hair laid perfectly all the time. For me this just isn't realistic - **don't get it twisted**, I do try, but I now accept that I cannot look perfect all the time. I remember how it feels to not be able to get your skin 'right' and be the one person who doesn't have the poppin' sun-kissed skin that influencers on social media seem to have so effortlessly. For years, I felt like I was in a battle with my skin and that I was never going to win, no matter how many new products I tried. But, slowly, I learnt how to love and care for my skin, and now **my glow is strong**.

Looking after your skin is such an important part of caring for your body, but learning what it needs isn't easy. Good skin takes time. There is so much information about skincare products and make-up brands out there, and everyone seems to have a different opinion on the best thing for your skin. But, on a basic level, even if you have acne, spots or dark marks there is **no such thing as bad skin**. You just need to clock what products work best for you,

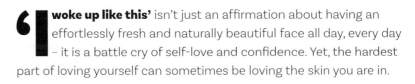

which routines to follow and – most importantly – to learn what doesn't work for you, even if that same product or remedy worked for everyone else. In this chapter, I am going to share some skincare tips with you and get you to think about how important it is to make the time to care for your skin.

But first, I'm going to have a much-needed conversation with you about **colourism**. We can't talk about 'good skin' without talking about the messages we are constantly sent about what 'good skin' means. When I'm talking with you about your skin, I'm talking about every part of it – the tone, the complexion and the texture. But I can't tell you to love your skin and treat it well and not address that, sometimes, the biggest issue many of us have with our skin is how dark it is. When I was younger, I felt like an ugly duckling. People would talk about how pretty my light-skinned friends or family members were, and I'd listen, knowing that I looked completely different from them. I knew that, often, when someone paid a compliment about nice skin, they were not talking about how it glowed or how clear that person's complexion was – they were talking about how light it was. Whether these were throwaway comments or purposely hurtful statements, they stopped me from believing I was truly beautiful, and I want to make sure you don't have the same experience. For a long time, I believed I wasn't beautiful simply because I was a Black girl – I was always waiting for someone to tell me I was pretty or for a boy to show me attention so that I could believe I was attractive. I wasted so much time seeking approval and validation from others. But I want you to know that you don't have to wait for someone else to tell you that you are beautiful for you to know that you are. Remember, my skin is my beauty and **your skin is your beauty**, and that will never change.

> *'Finally I realised that beauty was not a thing that I could acquire or consume, it was something that I just had to be.'*
> **Lupita Nyong'o** [2]

Loving the skin you're in

Loving your skin is about loving every inch of it, including your skintone. **Let's be real**, we have largely been taught that white (or light) skin and European features are the most beautiful, and that looking like a fair-skinned 'browning' is what we should all be aiming for. We are fed this message consciously and subconsciously every day by adverts, Instagram influencers, TV programmes and sometimes even by our own family. It feels like every rap song has a line about how beautiful 'lighties' or 'redbones' are, and we just don't see people coming with that same energy when it comes to **celebrating Black women** of every hue.

Black women are seen as less beautiful by society, and the darker we are, the less beautiful society tells us we are. It isn't just about what we see in the media. Around the world and throughout history, the darker people's skins are, the more discrimination they have suffered. Over generations, through colonialism and through slavery, we have been taught that the 'ideal' is to be close to whiteness, and that the lighter your skin is the more acceptable you are. But open discussions about this are still not commonplace. Instead, we learn to internalise a dislike for dark skin and have come to expect the stories of Black women being brutalised and openly called less beautiful or less worthy. We hear it when an aunty asks us why we are so dark compared to our lighter sisters, or when someone makes a joke about our skin, our nose or our lips, or laughs at how 'Black' we are to our faces or on social media.

Even as a hardback, grown, Black woman, I can still get caught up and start to question myself and my beauty when I see these colourist messages over and over again. When I was younger, this didn't just affect how I felt about myself, it affected how I felt about my friends too. I will never forget when I was on the train and someone mentioned how pretty my friend Kristina was, and I replied, 'Yeah, she rocks it well for a dark-skin girl.' At the time, I didn't know how damaging this was, but I look back with such disappointment in myself. **How could I have let these ideas seep into my mind without even realising?!** I had to work to undo all the negative perceptions I had taken in about dark skin not being beautiful, and I really had to think about why I would even say something like that about someone I really loved.

It goes deeper than who is beautiful and who isn't. Colourism does more than just tear down the confidence of dark-skinned women – within the insidious structures of racism, it makes them the most vulnerable of all. Black women with darker skin are often stereotyped as being more aggressive, ignorant, 'ghetto' or 'ratchet'. They statistically face more violence and more discrimination the world over. That is why the so-called 'jokes' made by high-profile celebrities and influencers comparing dark-skinned women to animals or reinforcing negative stereotypes are so dangerous. **These aren't just 'jokes'** – they are hurtful, they are discriminatory, they cause people emotional trauma and they **aren't acceptable.** And for the record, it doesn't matter how badly you may or may not have been treated by a dark-skinned girl – you don't have permission to spread hate or colourism.

> *'Colourism is the daughter of racism.'*
> **Lupita Nyong'o** [3]

When talking about the experiences of dark-skinned women, I am not saying that lighter-skinned women do not face racial discrimination or always have it easier. But there is a difference in their experiences. **Acknowledging the difficulties of our sisters doesn't take away from our own struggles**, it simply gives us a better perspective on the lives of other Black women around us. You should always challenge people who have negative things to say about being dark-skinned or feel the need to comment on how 'Black' someone is. Only by openly rejecting these attitudes can we expect things to **change in our community.**

We need to talk about why so much value is tied to the lightness of our skin. Not only would I encourage you to call out colourism when you see it, but also to turn your gaze inwards and focus on what you like about your own skin. Remind yourself – and your dark-skinned sisters – that you are **beautiful**. I know it's hard to feel that way when you are being bullied or dragged down for something that you cannot change, but the first step is accepting yourself.

If you are struggling to love your skin, let's set out some affirmations below that you can say out loud each and every time you feel low about your skin.

Use the space below to write down three things you like about your skin – scars, blemishes and all. Write statements you can repeat to yourself easily.

1. ....
....
....

2. ....
....
....

3. ....
....
....

If you are struggling to find confidence in your skin, print off pictures of beautiful women with a similar skin tone to you and put them up on your wall, keep them in your journal or even set them as the background on your phone. Here are some suggestions: **Kelly Rowland, Gabrielle Union, Ari Lennox, Zuri Tibby, Leomie Anderson, Ray BLK, Danielle Brooks, Ms Banks, Laverne Cox, Adut Akech, JT, Anok Yai** and **Lizzo**. Look at these women and remind yourself daily how beautiful your brown skin is.

'Your deep mahogany skin may not resemble that of the others in your family ... One day you'll appreciate how much your brown skin shines in the moonlight, glistens in the Sun and ages ever so slowly.'
Gabrielle Union [4]

TRUE STORY

I had terrible acne when I was a teenager. It was so bad that I struggle to even look at pictures of myself from my teenage years to this day. To be honest, I cut most of them up and dashed them away once I'd **glowed up** and acne was no longer my portion. At thirteen, my face was officially a problem – every day I would wake up with a new rash or spot or have even more marks on my skin from where I had picked at blemishes (even though I tried so badly not to touch them). My forehead was so bumpy and congested it actually resembled rocky road chocolate. I was so paranoid about what my friends or the boys I was into would think about the spots on my face, and I dreaded going to school. With my acne, braces, messy hair and nerdy glasses, I literally hated looking at myself and I felt so ugly. And even though I got skin products from doctors, nothing seemed to work.

To make things worse, everyone around me seemed to have the clearest skin. (This is probably an exaggeration, but I felt really alone.) The comments people made about my skin **cut me deep**. If you are lucky enough not to have blemishes, try to be understanding. Do not tease people about their spots. This is something they cannot change and they are probably already self-conscious about it. Try to have compassion for others and treat them the way you would want to be treated, because none of us are perfect.

Other people tried to be helpful and offer 'advice', but it was just annoying that everyone had something to say about me having acne or scars on my face. I never went around asking for help – I was just praying no one would notice how blemished my skin was. And a lot of the time they didn't. The thing is, while we are super sensitive about each imperfection and mark on our faces, it's likely that other people won't notice because they are too busy worrying and stressing about their own.

Words matter

Your skin is yours to love, regardless of any issue it has. You should never say you hate your skin or that you have bad skin – words are powerful, so please use them to **uplift yourself**. Keep a positive attitude towards your skin – you *will* learn how to manage it, and it *will* get better. Sometimes, you need to talk da tings dem! Speak clear, healthy skin into existence and protect your self-worth by praising your skin even if it's going through a bad patch.

Let's talk skincare

Now, Mel and I aren't experts on skincare, but we are out here trying to be **Rich Aunty Skin Goals** and have picked up a few tips along the way. These pointers will start you off on your skincare journey – they are not the be-all and end, all but we've all gotta start somewhere …

First things first, take a few minutes to answer these questions about your skin.

What do I know about how to look after my skin?

....

What do I use to wash my face?

....

How often do I carve out time to care for my skin?

....

It is hard to look after your skin if you are not sure what it needs. When I was younger, I didn't really understand that there are different skin types, so I tried to use the harshest products to kill any blemishes and erase any dark acne scars ASAP. But what I really needed to do was learn more about my skin so that I could look after it properly and prevent breakouts in the first place. So, use the questions below to get to know yours a bit better, and then I'll talk you through the different skin types.

What's my biggest skin concern?

....

How does my skin feel after I have washed it?

....

How does my skin feel at the end of the day?

....

Where do I usually get excess shine, spots, pimples or blackheads?

....

That's my type ...

There are five common skin types: **normal, oily, dry, combination** and **sensitive**. To put it simply, your skin type is determined by how much oil the pores on your face produce. You can have two or more types of skin on your face – for example, you might produce a lot of oil around your nose and chin, but your cheeks are really dry.

Normal skin isn't too oily, too sensitive or too dry – it's well-balanced.

Oily skin is usually shiny and gets greasy throughout the day. You may have blackheads, pimples or other spots on your face. (Type tip: try to use oil-free or water-based products.)

Dry skin can feel rough and look ashy. There might be areas that are flaky, scaly, peeling or itchy. Your skin can feel really tight after you have washed it. (Type tip: keep your skin hydrated by using a heavy-duty moisturiser overnight.)

Combination skin is a mix of skin types. Usually, your T-zone (the forehead, nose and chin) is oily but the skin on your cheeks is dry. However, there could be other combinations as well.

BIG FACT

It doesn't mean that your skin is a problem if you don't have a 'normal' skin type, it just means you need targeted products that suit your skin better.

What type of skin do you think you have?

....

....

Work that routine

On a basic level, if you want healthy skin, you need to treat it well. Even if you have a perfectly clear complexion, you still need to look after it to keep it that way. When I was young, I never understood how important it was to set aside time to look after myself, and when it came to caring for my skin, I just saw it as something I needed to get done, not something I should take time to enjoy. Remember, **you are the prize**. You deserve to give yourself the best, and sometimes that means simply giving your skin the time, care and attention it deserves. You cannot have a higgi hagga approach – you have to be consistent in order to see results.

I am going to give you a few tips on what a good skincare routine looks like, but it really depends on what works for you. Just know that you don't need a complicated routine with loads of products and steps.

The backbone of every skincare routine is a **cleanser**, which you should use twice a day. You need to wash your skin at night before you go to bed to prevent the oil, dirt and pollution you've been exposed to throughout the day from building up and clogging up your pores. Then you need to wash it again in the morning to free it of any sweat and oil that may have accumulated while you were sleeping. Even if you don't do anything else I suggest in this chapter, cleansing twice a day can help prevent spots, acne and greasy skin.

The next product you can add to your routine is a **toner**. A toner's job is to give your skin an extra cleanse, refresh it and provide some additional hydration. It should be used after you cleanse and before you moisturise.

This brings me on to **moisturiser**. A moisturiser's job is to stop your skin from drying out. It can also help protect your skin from the environment, as it creates a barrier that keeps oils from escaping and harmful outside elements, such as pollution, from getting in.

Once you have that covered, you can add in a weekly **face mask**. Face masks should be applied after you've cleansed your face and removed any make-up. They work by allowing your pores to really soak up the product. There are many different types of masks that target different issues you may be experiencing with your skin, from deep cleansers to soothing balms for irritated or sensitive skin. For me, the best thing about wearing a mask is that it allows me to rest and relax for twenty minutes while giving my skin the attention it needs.

If you suffer from breakouts, you can also use specific **spot creams** to help calm inflammation and prevent new blemishes forming. These products are best used overnight, as your skin heals fastest while you are sleeping. If your acne is persistent, it might be a good idea to seek the opinion of a skincare professional or a doctor to see what other treatments are available. Be aware that some spot creams can make your skin more sensitive to the Sun, which leads me to my next point …

Wear SPF. SPF protects your skin from the Sun's harmful ultraviolet light. There are two types of ultraviolet light – **UVA** and **UVB**. UVA causes skin damage, skin aging and wrinkles. UVB causes sunburn and plays a key role in the development of skin cancer cells. Everyone should be wearing SPF every day, no matter what their skin tone. Try and look for a product that protects against both UVA and UVB.

There are so many other things you can add to your routine, but don't rush to use products you might not even need. When I started with my first skincare routine, I used a cleanser, toner and moisturiser all from the same brand that were designed to work together to clear up my blemishes. I also bought a face mask to deep cleanse my skin once a week. Once I'd adjusted to those products and started to see a difference in my skin, I bought other products from the same brand and slowly worked them into my routine. You don't have to stick to the same brand though, and you'll probably have to experiment before you find products that work for you. The key thing is to try them out one at a time and remember there are no quick fixes for your skin – you need to **respect it and care for it**. Don't be impatient if you try a new product and you don't see results the same day. **Good things tek time, and so does great skin.**

Skincare is self-love

Ibi Meier-Oruitemeka,
founder of The Afro Hair & Skin Co.

Cultivating a daily skincare ritual is an important expression of self-love. In these moments, we can slow down, centre and uplift ourselves. This ritual is a physical expression of gratitude to our body, our home. An affirmation of self that shows we are worthy of rest, love and tenderness. As we cleanse, we wash away the day, both physically and energetically. Renewing the skin. A face mask charged with the Earth's potent minerals can relax and ground us while enhancing our skin's texture. The act of massaging oils, helps to nourish and and balance our skin, boost the blood flow and replenish our glow. Looking after our skin can revive us.

Watch your mouth

When it comes to your skin, what you put inside your body matters just as much as what you put on it. **Your skin is your body's largest organ, and you get the best out of it when you give it the best fuel.** Eating certain foods can have a bad impact on your skin and make breakouts worse. Every person is different, so it might take some trial and error to figure out what foods can trigger your breakouts – but, it's a good idea to be aware of what you're putting in your mouth and how it affects your glow.

I had never made the connection between my skin and what I ate and drank until I met a lady at the post office who told me to eat fruit to help my skin improve. (Yes, that's how bad my skin was – so bad that well-intentioned strangers would give me tips on how to fix it.) I was upset at what she said, but I thought I might as well try it – and actually worked for me. Now, if I'm ever having a breakout, I try to avoid processed and sugary foods and dairy products because I've found that eating them makes things worse for me. Don't get me wrong, I LOVE FOOD – it is my main comfort, so when I am feeling bad the first thing I want to do is treat myself – but I know that if my skin is going through a bad spell, eating isn't isn't going to help.

To keep your skin glowing, try to eat a lot of fresh fruit, vegetables, fish and nuts. I know it's hard, but try to cut back on cakes, chocolate, biscuits, fried foods and sugar. You don't have to give these things up completely, you just need to have some balance. Why not try cutting down on them for two weeks and see what happens? Then you can see whether it changed the way your skin looks and feels. Once I did this and actually started seeing results, I never looked back – and now I don't even check for chocolate and crisps the way I used to.

Water is life

Drink up! There are so many health benefits linked to drinking lots of water, and it really is the plug for healthy skin. If you don't drink enough, you will get dehydrated and your skin will suffer. If you want soft, smooth skin, water is your friend. We take in a lot of toxins through the food we eat and the pollution in the air around us, but thankfully drinking enough water can flush out these toxins.

TIPS
If you have bad acne, adding more nuts into your diet may help. Nuts contain selenium, which is a great protective nutrient for healthy skin. If you can't eat nuts, you can also get selenium from eggs, sunflower seeds, tuna and mushrooms.

Vitamin C is a MAJOR KEY. It helps brighten your skin, protects it from pollution and promotes a natural glow.

TIPS
If you don't like drinking water, you can add chopped fresh fruits to give it a bit of flavour and get a vitamin boost at the same time. When I need something sweet, I put some strawberries in my water bottle. Water is good for us, but it can get boring.

Don't touch your spots

Hello, hello, hi! Please do not pick, pop or squeeze your spots! Or let anyone else dig out your spots – even your babes. Trust me, I know it's hard to keep your hands away. Each time I see a spot on my face, it's like everything else fades into the darkness and this spot (which probably isn't even that big) is now the only thing I see – and the rest of the world when they look at me. But this really is all in my head. **Don't obsess over a new spot.** Touching and worrying your spots does not get rid of them, it only makes them more painful, more obvious and can leave scars on your beautiful face. As Black people, we are more likely to suffer from hyperpigmentation – a condition that causes our skin to overproduce melanin. Melanin is what gives our skin, hair and eyes their colour. Any irritation to our skin (including cuts and rashes) can cause dark marks to form, which can sometimes take months to fade. **It's not worth the drama.** Leave. It. Alone.

BIG FACT

If it is getting to a point where you are constantly breaking out and suffering from pimples all over your face, speak to your doctor. Acne and breakouts are a part of life, but if it is too much for you or you suspect it's a sign of something more serious (like an allergy) there are many different medications and creams that can help to control it. Your body will go through a lot of hormonal changes and sometimes you will need a little bit of help, and that's OK.

If you really want to get rid of pimples quickly, try applying a little tea tree oil (I said a LITTLE) and use a spot cream as part of your night-time routine. Accept that for the next few days the spot will be there, and continue to apply the spot cream each night. Very soon it will shrink and, if you haven't picked it, you should have survived a pimple without scarring your face.

Treat your skin with love

Kadian Pow, founder and Chief Mixologist of Bourn Beautiful Naturals

When I was a teenager, I suffered from acne. I was very hard on my skin, approaching the eradication of acne as if I were going to war. I used harsh alcohol toners, rough physical exfoliants and acidic blemish zappers. They did not work. Instead, I was left with skin that was unbalanced and raw, and I felt like a failure. What I did begin to learn until my late twenties and early thirties, was that approaching my skin with love was the best possible thing I could have done. Focus on the science of your skin's behaviour instead of product promises. Don't try to conquer your skin into submission, but love it into acceptance.

We DON'T bleach and we DON'T entertain it

I have talked about how difficult it can be to love and take care of your skin, but there is one thing that is a definite no-no, and that's bleaching. **There is absolutely no justification for bleaching your skin.** Your skin is beautiful whatever shade it is, and you should never use any product to try and lighten it. I get it, hyperpigmentation is real and it isn't nice to have dark marks or dark circles under your eyes, but there is a big difference between trying to lighten a few dark marks here and there and trying to change your skin tone completely.

Lightening creams are filled with harmful ingredients that will not only damage your skin, but can have terrible effects on your overall health too. They can cause your skin to flake, burn, look uneven and can even leave permanent scars. One of the main ingredients in most bleaching creams is mercury, and mercury is POISONOUS. **Nothing is worth poisoning yourself for.**

Plus, these products are actually illegal. It might not seem that way because you can still go to your local hair shop and pick them off the shelf, or ask for even stronger creams over the counter – and there are so many brands that sell and market bleaching creams in other countries too. But just know that the people selling these bleaching creams are breaking the law.

Remember, **you are BEAUTIFUL** no matter what shade your skin is. You don't need to put your life at risk just to meet a false standard of beauty. Black skin is regal – as a Black woman, I am blessed with my Black skin, and I wear my beauty daily with pride and honour. I urge you to own your beauty and your skintone too – carry yourself with confidence in your gloriously melanated, glowing skin.

If you hate the shade of your skin and feel under pressure to bleach it, talk to someone you trust – it could be a big sister, a friend, an aunty or even your GP. You aren't the only one feeling like this and you might benefit from counselling or extra support to get to a place where you truly love your skin. There is no shame in this – self-love is a journey and if you need help, you must ask for it.

The skin you are in

Audrey Indome co-host of The Receipts podcast

Growing up in a predominantly white area meant that I often felt invisible, but I wish I had spent more time loving the skin I'm, in – instead of wasting time hating it. Your melanin is your magic, and the sooner you accept this the better. Self-love is a marathon and not a sprint. Remember that, and you'll be just fine.

Keep going

The most important skincare tip I can give you is to **love your skin** - every part of it. Treat it with care, give it time, and be positive about your skincare journey. Do not let periods of bad acne or hyperpigmentation lower your confidence.

"I'm Black, I'm dark and I'm [...] beautiful." **Michaela Coel** [5]

Remember, if you are feeling low, say your affirmations and try not to compare your skin to others around you. **Everyone is on their own journey**, make sure you focus on yours.

Continue to **educate yourself**. The conversations about colourism we have started in this chapter need to continue, and we have a long way to go to tackle the harmful impact colourism has on our community – everyone has a part to play in challenging the negative perceptions about dark skin. **Remember to love yourself, love your skin and love your sisters.**

Crowning glory

A love letter to Black hair

By Melissa

Lotion. Oil. Creams. Curls, coils, kinks and cotton. Waves. Locs and braids. The intricate canerows that take four hours to create. Slicked-back bun. Middle parting. Chiney bumps. Your first silk press. Thirty-inch weave. 613 bundles. Frontals. Fulani braids, Finger waves. Black gel. Dipping the ends of your braids in hot water. Baby hairs and an old toothbrush to swoop, slick and style. Ribbons. Barrettes and beads. Your girlfriends screaming, 'What lace?'. Hair bobbles. Your mum bumping the ends of your hair so you don't look grown. A bal''ead. Colourful headwraps. Du-rags. Shrinkage. Hijabs. Colourful braids during school summer holidays. The smell of hair grease. Sweating out your hair. Big afro puffs that block people's view. Looking for your bonnet before bed. Or a silk pillow if you're bougie like that. Sleeping with your head propped on a pillow so you don't ruin your style. Washing your hair over the bath. Straighteners burning. The conk on the back of your head from your mum's comb. Deep conditioning your hair being a whole event. Your first visit to the hairdressers.

> '*What I've learned from myself is that I don't have to be anybody else. Myself is good enough.*'
> Lupita Nyong'o [1]

SLICK. TEASE. DEFINE

This chapter is an ode to the beauty, diversity and tenacity of how we style or cover Black hair. They say, 'the bigger the hair, the closer to God', but for me – no matter its thickness, length or how you choose to present it – **your hair is your crowning glory.**

My hair determines a lot of what I do and how I feel. Whether it's going swimming, deciding if I should exercise or if a night out raving is worth sweating out my silk press. Sometimes, if I can't get my edges to lay flat my mood will just flatline. I'll be big mad. **But when I'm having a good hair day, you can't tell me nothing!** I even walk differently. When Natalie and I decide to produce an event, the first thing we ask each other isn't, 'How much will this cost?' or 'Who is coming?'; it's, 'What are you wearing?', 'Which wig this time?' or 'Shall we do braids or an afro puff?'. Hair care is self-care for me. Buying a new wig, picking out my 'fro or slicking back my hair so I can attach a water wave ponytail is one of the first things I do when I feel low or want to look good.

As a child, having my hair washed and my scalp greased on a Sunday afternoon before school – sat in between my mother's knees as she parted the hair on my scalp – was almost a spiritual moment. As she combed out single strand knots and massaged my scalp, she nurtured and uplifted me, offering up affirmations as she listened to my problems and offered advice. We weren't regular church goers, but a Sunday was always a day of reflection, and it was in these moments that I felt most connected to my mother.

My mum would re-tell funny stories until we were on the floor cackling with laughter. This was like therapy for me. Discussing things like politics and family drama. Passing on family history and traditions. Or my mum explaining why I should read my books rather than focus on boys. I didn't realise it at the time, but my mum was silently teaching me and showing me the way through these sessions. Letting me know what it meant to be grown.

Storytelling and hair care go hand in hand, and those Sunday Salon Sessions were where my mum first told me about her life. Using those quiet moments to not only explain things to me, but to allow me the opportunity to express myself unapologetically. **As Black people we are natural storytellers.** It is a tradition that has been passed down through history: whether it was through the medium of song to provide enslaved people with messages that would lead them to freedom; or our parents using proverbs like, 'Those who don't listen must feel' to further emphasise an experience; or parables used as cautionary tales to communicate important lessons; or bussin' jokes with your hairdresser whilst she spills the tea. From Anansi stories to Twitter stories, we continue to pass on important messages through the use of story tales.

As I got older, I began to share similar experiences with friends. One of my favourite things to do was spend my Saturdays with my BFF Tameka. We used the day to cater to ourselves. Taking care of what we felt was important. The first thing we would do is go to Finsbury Park and wander through the aisle of a hair shop, trying to find the perfect products to emulate the styles we had seen in our favourite music videos. This might be trying to get the exact same colour weave as Ciara had in the 'Goodies' video, or trying to figure out how Brandy's braids stayed so neat. (It was a wig!)

Whether it was purchasing gel, pink or a yaky ponytail, we would spend ages in that shop, laughing, joking and spilling secrets as we searched for the right product. We would make sure we also picked up one of the fruity rollerball lip glosses or the thick sticky 99p clear glosses to complete our look. With our hair catered to, our next step was finding something to educate our minds. We definitely couldn't be grown without reading a book or two, so off we went to New Beacon Books. As the UK's first Black publisher and specialist bookshop, it was the only place I knew where I could find books that centred people that looked like me. After that, we would buy patties, a can of Ting for me and Rio for Tameka. Back then that's all I needed to feel good. **Hair products, lip gloss, books and a pattie – Black Girl Joy personified.**

Now as a big woman, things have hardly changed. The only difference is I pay people to do my hair for me! For many of us, the hairdressers is an institution. When I was younger – despite the hours I spent there – the hairdressers was the place I loved going to feel grown, pretending to read my book as I listened to big people business. As an adult, it was the one place for me that was outside of the white gaze. Where else could I go and off my wig? Or would I be willing to show where my edges had broken off? It's where what's 'cool' or 'in' was dictated by people who look just like me. **In the Black hairdressers, you are the mainstream and so your self-esteem and image of yourself can be restored from the pressures of everyday life.** No hairstyle is unachievable. Your hair is never too short to pick up and braid. An aunty will swoop your fringe, slick it down and give you that high pony of your dreams. Even if you don't have enough bundles, that's OK – they will try a ting and have you looking and feeling sensational.

As a Black woman, your hairdresser or barber is one of the most trusted people in your life – who else would you let use shears, scissors or toxic chemicals so close? You rely on them not to braid too tight, cut your hair too short and not to leave you under the dryer for hours as they eat their lunch or argue with their man. A good hairdresser will become like family. From squeezing you in if you need a late-night appointment, to providing you with an extra bundle when your AliExpress delivery doesn't come through.

'[Hair] was a way of connecting with other black girls ... I would braid friends' hair and it would always be something I could talk about culturally.'
Gina Knight [2]

When I think back to those Sunday afternoons, when my mum would do my hair, I see the way in which Black Hair Culture has been passed down through the generations. **There's a special fellowship, solidarity and camaraderie that is borne out of entrusting someone to do your hair.** Doing your hair can take hours, sometimes days. So, it's a process that encourages bonding. I get the same feeling when someone I don't know shares their favourite product with me. It's real community – trust and togetherness in those moments. Like when a friend nices me by sharing the number of the aunty that does braids. But not just any aunty – the one that doesn't ask you to separate and hand her the hair attachment as she braids your hair!

When I'm feeling down, nothing beats getting my hair done with all of the other customers hailing me up and telling me how good I look. It's why we called our first Black Girls' Book Club festival the Salon - a play on a literary salon and the hair salon. A salon is a gathering of people led by an engaging and inspiring host. Anyone who has had the pleasure of having their hair braided by an aunty for six hours knows just how much of a big personality the best hairdressers have. Just like a hair salon, a literary salon draws people into engaging and amusing conversations and raucous debates. It's a real meeting of minds. No matter whether you agree or disagree with the point being made, you leave that experience feeling edified, having had the opportunity to increase your knowledge and understanding through heated conversation and loud debate. **The Salon gives you permission to be yourself.**

The politics of Black hair: style vs. substance

When I liken Black hair care practices to spiritual experiences, I'm not just being extra. It's an acknowledgement that the way we care for our hair, and the politics surrounding it, is much more than just fashion and style. It's part of our rich history. Whether that means growing locs, choosing to wear a covering such as a hijab or wearing a veil for your confirmation, hair is so

'Our hair is the highest point on our entire body, and therefore considered most connected to the divine. In some degree our hair was supposed to grow up ... as a way to connect to the spiritual world
Dr Afiya Mbilishaka [3]

important to many belief systems. Just looking at someone's hair could tell you something about their identity. The braids themselves can tell a story. Elaborate braiding patterns were created to indicate different purposes, from people attending ceremonies and weddings, to those going to war. Adding jewels, shells and beads to those braids would indicate things such as status, or whether a girl had transitioned into womanhood.

As some of the most trusted members of society, braiders were often the most senior female members of the family, and they passed their techniques onto their daughters as a way of keeping those traditions alive. That phrase I quoted earlier, 'The higher the hair, the closer to God', isn't just a joke about having big hair that grows up and out. Your head being the most elevated part of your body meant that it was closer to the skies, ensuring that not only was your hair a channel for spiritual interaction, it was a way for spirits to reach your soul.

Braids and canerowed styles were traditionally a marker of identity. They were used to indicate a person's wealth, age, religion, social position, tribe or even marital status. Through the contours of their hair, enslaved people used the designs to send messages by mapping out routes to freedom or they hid seeds and grain underneath hair strands as a means of survival. These styles weren't just protective because they ensured good hair care – they were a means of keeping us alive. Black hair tells the story of survival.

So, when I say it's spiritual. I mean it! The things I do to style my hair. The people I allow to take care of it. Physically. Mentally. Spiritually. It's all so intrinsically linked to how I take care of me. **Taking care of my hair care is my form of self-care.**

As a Black girl, you will already know just how important Black Hair Culture is – either from watching your mum spending all afternoon in the hairdressers, or from attempting to lay your edges or picking out your afro puffs in the mornings before school. The way in which you choose to wear your hair can be seen as an expression of your style, a declaration of your religious beliefs or a statement about your politics. While you are busy trying to figure out who you are, what you like, what you stand for and where you see yourself, playing with your hair and switching up your style is a simple – yet effective – way of personal expression and evolution.

'My cotton crown blooms coiled antennas, each having the individuality of snowflakes.'
Sylene 'SylJoe' Joseph [4]

I've often found that different hairstyles dictate how I am treated and how people respond to me. Natural hairstyles are often seen as a symbolism of my Blackness, or even a rejection of the mainstream. People call me 'sis' or give me extra oxtail gravy on my food if I'm wearing my hair in an afro puff. But 99.9 per cent of the time, I style my hair in a particular way because I think it looks cute, not because I want to start a revolution.

Throughout history, Black women's hair has been on the lips of anyone and everyone that has had the pleasure to view it. Sometimes, the focus on Black hair inside and outside of the community can be overwhelming. Dodging the hands of those who desperately want to touch it. Being forced to grin and bear it when a stylist says that, because of its texture, it needs to be blown out before they can even look at it. Your hair, and how you choose to style it, can conjure up a whole heap of feelings.

Others will project their thoughts about Black hair onto you. The culture of anti-Blackness has meant that often those outside of our community – who do not have similar textures or hair practices – believe they have the right to determine how we wear our hair, despite the fact that they have no business doing so. People have always tried to dictate how we wear our hair – from the headwraps enforced on us after emancipation, to schools labelling Black hair 'distracting', 'unruly' or 'wild', and to the pressure. to look 'presentable' by adopting straight hairstyles when entering the world of work. Our natural hairstyles are seen as inappropriate or unprofessional unless someone else does it first.

Fighting for hair equality in the classroom

Ruby Williams (she/her), university student, make up artist, hair equality campaigner and consultant and volunteer at 'No More Exclusions' - an abolitionist coalition set up to end race disparities in schools

Ruby first took on institutional racism and hair discrimination after being sent home from school on multiple occasions. Her crime? Her hair grew up and out, rather than down. Here, Mel talks to her about her experience.

Mel: Why did you choose to fight your school for your right to wear your Afro hair?

Ruby: I chose to fight the rule about afro hair in my school because I thought it was really unfair that only pupils with afro hair were being forced to cut, chemically alter or hide their hair in order to attend school. The schools policy specifically mentioned that afro hair had to be of a 'reasonable' size and length, but made no mention of rules or regulations for pupils with straighter hair textures. I knew the rule was wrong, so I wanted to fight it for myself and for all the other pupils with afro hair who were in that school, and for the younger children who would attend after me.

Mel: How did you go from being repeatedly sent home from school over your hair to being a Hair Equality campaigner?

Ruby: Hackney Council and Education Authority were horrified about what had happened to me, and they promised to share guidelines with all Hackney schools about the type of hair rules they should have. They met with me, my parents and other people who had had this experience. They also included other schools in the conversation. One local school has since got rid of their hair rules altogether. They also encouraged all Hackney schools to celebrate World Afro Day in September 2020. The policies aren't complicated, they simply remind schools of their legal duties regarding the Equality Act 2010, and how hair rules shouldn't unfairly impact specific groups of pupils. I hope schools listen to them so nobody else faces what I went through.

Mel: What is your relationship with your hair like now? Is there a particular hairstyle that empowers you since this experience?

Ruby: Even throughout this experience, I managed to keep a positive relationship with my hair. I knew that it was the school in the wrong, not me or my hair. I love changing my look, depending on how I feel, and I will experiment with different styles. In the summer I loved trying knotless box braids with a golden brown highlight through them. They were really long and looked so different to how my own hair usually is so it was a nice change! I don't think I really have a favourite style. As Black and mixed-heritage girls we are spoilt for choice!

Mel: Is there something you wish every Black girl could know?

Ruby: I want every Black and mixed-race person to know that their hair is their crown and something they should be proud of. They should feel the freedom to choose to wear it in whatever way helps them feel confident and comfortable. Do not let anyone else tell you how you should wear your crown – and we should also make sure we are not judging others about their choices too.

Discrimination against Black hair isn't just happening in Britain. It happens across the Black diaspora, to people of African ancestry around the world. **Even in majority Black countries.**

Over twenty years ago, celebrated Jamaican poet, author and broadcaster Joan Andrea Hutchinson wrote the poem *Dat Bumpyheaded Gal* in response to being cussed, chastised and made fun of for daring to wear her natural hair in chiney bumps on television. As a young girl, I only wore chiney bumps to air dry my hair, but I always felt **pride** when I saw women like Mel B, Rihanna and Naomi Campbell **rocking them in public.** Those little twisted buns were an intentional display of their Blackness. But the reaction to Ms Hutchinson was not that of pride. The Jamaican public complained, saying things like, 'tek dat dutty bumpy head gyal, dat nasty looking dutty head gyal off the TV'. But for Ms Hutchinson, **respectability politics** is so embedded into the fabric of Jamaica's consciousness that what could have been seen as a moment of pride and celebration – a dark-skinned Black woman proudly wearing her hair in a familiar, natural style – led to **condemnation, uproar and disgust.**

> **Respectability politics is a belief that conforming to 'mainstream' standards of appearance and behaviour will ensure that you face less prejudice. But this is not true. Looking or behaving a certain way isn't a cheat code – wearing your hair in a straighter style or wearing church shoes isn't going to protect you from society's anti-Blackness.**

Ms Hutchinson's poem, 'Dat Bumpyhead Gal' is an ode to Black beauty in all its forms. Not only does it break down the many ways in which the way our hair grows naturally out of our head is weaponised and used against us, it also does so in a familiar language – patois. Further emphasising that who you are doesn't have to be moulded or changed to fit society's ideals of what is proper and correct. **Rather than accept these negative comments, Ms Hutchinson threw them back and declared that she loves the skin she's in.**

DAT BUMPYHEAD GAL
JOAN ANDREA HUTCHINSON[5]

Tell mi say mi no good enough fi you TV screen
How mi offend you eyesight
Tell mi say mi is a black, ugly, bumpyhead gal
And mi tell you, mi feeling right

Cuss mi say mi is a bootoo, and mi no have no class
Trace mi and galang rude
Tell mi say a educated woman shoulda know better
And I tell you mi feeling good

You say mi hairstyle disgusting chaka chaka an tan bad
And favour like something out a street
And say mi should a shame fi lef mi house tan so
And mi smile, for mi feeing sweet

You see, the truth is, mi not ashamed of mi owna self
Mi not afraid of me
When mi look into the mirror, mi like the somebody
Weh mi see a look pon me

Mi like her thick nappy hair and her broad face
Mi like her in and out of clothes
But most of all mi love weh she stan up for and defend
And, a no pose she a pose

But serious, when you a go fall in love with you
And leggo of all you fear
When you ago take the time tell God thanks fi you life
Instead of fret bout 'hair'

For if it kinky or straight, if it black or white
Transparent or opaque
God make all a wi fi a special reason
And God don't make mistake

So if you want to criticize the Father work
Then you life going to be 'salt'
For the Creator love all a wi and look out fi wi
Even when wi have plenty fault

So galang, call mi black and bumpyhead if you want
But make sure say you say it loud
Because the Creator love me and me feel good
Fi be bumpyhead, black and proud.

Black hair politics isn't as simple as someone being 'advised' to wear their hair in a different style. It's the looks. The name calling. 'Bad', 'picky', 'nappy', 'tough' or 'chaka chaka' being used as an insult for tighter-coiled or kinkier hair. Being told your hair is 'wild' or 'unprofessional'. The expectation that your hair will feel like a wiry brillo pad when it's touched. **Without permission.** The shock and surprise when it isn't. Can we deep the lack of respect and sheer audacity it takes for someone to take their dry, ashy, unwashed hands and touch your hair as if you were an animal in the zoo?

That's why the conversations surrounding cultural appropriation are important. As Black girls, you have to fight to simply be able to wear the hair that grows out of your own head in peace. Some people don't understand why cultural appropriation stings so much. But when people are appropriating our styles and repackaging them back to us – such as Kim K's 'boxer braids', or companies that reinvent the silk bonnet and then try to sell it back to us for ten times the price – you can see why we're mad. It's the failure to understand that there is history,

'We create the culture that makes things 'cool', but the original is called 'ghetto' or 'urban'. It only becomes 'high fashion' when a non-Black stylist recreates it.'

Misa Hylton [6]

ritual and tradition that influence Black hair practices. It's the lack of acknowledgment that Black women and girls are called names for the way our hair grows out of head, and for the styles we wear. It's the fact that wearing our natural hair can get us expelled from school, but when your white or racially-ambiguous friends attempt to replicate canerow or braided styles, they are seen as cool, quirky and innovative. Or in Kim's case – the epitome of beauty and style.

Why I wrote My Hair

Hannah Lee (she/her), author

My Hair started life as a poem about the hair I lost as a teenager when I had cancer. I developed it into a children's book when my nephew was born and I realised that there weren't many books featuring characters that looked like him. I'd experienced that lack of representation as a child, but had thought that things had changed. To see that they hadn't was upsetting. I wrote *My Hair* because I wanted to give Black children a book that would speak to and celebrate them. I knew that hair would be a big part of that. Black people take such pride in our hair. Hair is not just a thing on our heads. Hair is our history. Black hair is community, Black hair is versatile, Black hair is beauty. It's a massive part of how we express ourselves.

That's my type

Every Black woman's hair is unique. From kinks, curls, puffs and waves to those of you who have naturally straight hair, we appreciate and celebrate the beauty of your hair in all its different states. But we do have to discuss the elephant in the room. I'm sure you were waiting for me to drop it. So, let's get into it. Quickly.

Natalie introduced you to colourism in her skin chapter. So, let's say hello to **texturism**, colourism's ugly little sister. Texturism is the idea that certain hair types are more beautiful or desirable than others. Just like you've heard people coo, 'She's pretty for a dark skin girl', I'm sure you have also heard, 'She's got good hair eeh' from a random aunty you don't even like. **This is where things get sticky.** Wanting or preferring a looser texture isn't always just about having hair that is more 'manageable' or easier to style. It's about understanding that presenting your hair in straighter styles deems you more acceptable in a society that constantly promotes Eurocentric standards of beauty. If there is such a thing as hair hierarchy in Western society, curly coils and bushy afros are often relegated to the bottom.

> **When you police Black hair you police our very existence.**

Presenting a straighter style in place of your natural texture can be the difference between being treated well at school, being given the same opportunities as your peers, and being allowed to freely walk around a shop without being followed by a suspicious assistant. So it's not surprising that there has always been a method of providing Black women with a straighter, sleeker, more palatable look.

But that ain't it sis. Despite what you may have been told, good hair is healthy hair. Let me repeat that one more time: **GOOD HAIR IS HEALTHY HAIR.** Hair isn't better because it's a looser texture or it's easier to get a comb through.

So, reject any thoughts that your hair is 'picky', 'nappy' or 'tough'. These words have traditionally been used as ways to 'other' us and make us feel uncomfortable or dissatisfied with the natural texture of our hair. Our hair isnt 'coarse' or 'unmanageable', and there is no such thing as 'good' hair. We don't need to assimilate, or to camouflage the very nature of our hair to fit in.

So, what are the different hair types?

Black hair comes in so many different forms and in so many textures. The most important thing you need to know is what type you have, and how to look after it.

Oprah's hairstylist created the 'typing system' as a way in which to classify hair, with letters and numbers used to differentiate between kinky or coily curls. Whilst not a definitive breakdown of all types of hair, the system has been widely used since the 1990s as a starting point for many of us as we start our hair-care journey.

'Let me correct the erroneous impression held by some that I claim to straighten hair. I deplore such an impression because I have always held myself out as a hair culturist. I grow hair.'
Madam C.J. Walker [7]

Now, it is important to note that many people see coil categorisation as a way of enforcing **hair hierarchy** and promoting texturism, and that's with good reason – any system that categorises or classifies as a means of identification is in danger of promoting **separatism and segregation.** Essentially, it encourages people to celebrate one texture over another. On the plus side, it allows you to find community with others who have a similar texture to you, allowing the opportunity to ask for **tips and tricks** to help with your hair care. Typing may not be great, but as you begin to figure out what type of hair you have it is a good place to start.

Is it dry? Do you have split ends? Is it fine? Is it really thick?

With this in mind, rather than just focusing on the type of hair you have, I asked a few friends (and some experts) to help me discuss their personal experiences with their hair.

On hair typing

Rachael Twumasi-Corson (she/her), co-founder of Afrocenchix, the first British hair-care brand specifically for afro hair

At best, hair typing can be a distraction; at worst, it can be damaging to people's self-esteem whilst further dividing the Black community. It is centred more on selling products and less on education. And it's all packaged under the guise of personalisation.

Andre Walker created the classification system to describe just how easy it was to straighten what is now categorised as Type 1 and Type 2 hair.

1 = straight, 2 = wavy, 3 = curly, 4 = kinky. Later, the letters 'a', 'b' and 'c' were added to the classification ('a' being the least wavy / curly / kinky, and 'c' being the waviest / curliest / kinkiest).

When describing curly or afro hair, someone may say 'I'm Type 3' or 'I'm Type 4', followed by the corresponding letter. But, in general, scientific literature simply differentiates hair as Caucasian, Asian and African, as this provides sufficient information about the structure of the hair, and makes it easy to identify differences between different hair types.

There are many hair myths, but all hair – regardless of its type and texture – needs moisture. All hair is made of keratin bundles (protein) joined by disulphide and hydrogen bonds. The only real difference between hair types is that afro hair needs oils to seal that moisture within the strands as it is difficult for sebum (the natural oil our scalps produce) to travel down curly hair shafts.

We founded Afrocenchix to force the industry to work for people like us – people who embrace the cultural importance of afro hair and want to look and feel their best without compromising their health. We use science-backed expertise to help our community learn about and love our hair.

The key to good hair-care is building regimes that work for your hair and lifestyle, with quality products actually made with your best interests in mind.

Wear it proud

So, now you know about different types of hair and how to take care of them, let's talk about the power of Black hair and the way we choose to style it. It's fun to be able to go from style to style, figuring out that signature look that defines you. Whatever it is you want to do, you should be able to do it without comments that make you feel self-conscious.

In the next few pages, you'll find words of wisdom from some brilliant, inspirational women about how their hair empowers them in whatever way they choose to wear and style it.

On wearing a hijab

Raifa Rafiq (she/her), private funds lawyer, arts critic, writer and multi-award-winning podcaster

My hijab is a very important part of my identity because wearing it is my decision. I wear it how I want to and where I want to. This agency that I have over what I put on myself reminds me that I have choices, and those choices can shape my life in a way that I want them to. Wearing the hijab is one of the many significant choices I have made that empowers me every time I step outside my house. Being confident in how you look often affects how you feel and your self esteem, so it's important for me to find power in my clothes and in my body.

On alopecia

Gina Knight (she/her), founder of the global and award-winning wig company, now known as the Wig Watch

It's my mission to take away the stigma behind female hair loss. Although I make wigs, I am a proud, bald woman who confidently wears wigs – not to hide, but to highlight the many versions of myself.

I discovered I had alopecia when I had my first child in 2012. Postpartum shedding is a normal part of pregnancy, however, mine became very severe as I was losing chunks of hair at the crown and sides of my head. Getting a diagnosis was an uphill struggle. I was dismissed by GPs and told my hair loss in essence was my fault. It wasn't. It took a long time to discover I had alopecia, and, after doing my own research, I learned that this was common in many women.

After years of trying to hide my bald patches, I finally shaved my head in 2018. I was tired of trying to conceal my hairloss 24/7.

Wigs allow me to be versatile, and are easy to care for. My favourite wig is the YeMaia. I always feel glamorous when I wear her. All my wigs have Yoruba names and this one is named after my friends Maia and Yemaya – the Yorùbá Orisha (goddess) of the ocean. Growing up in foster care with white parents, I always felt a lack of connection to my Nigerian heritage. As I got older, I researched and became interested in the Yoruba legends – it's a way for me to gently nod at a culture I have often viewed from the outside looking in.

Even though I love my wigs, and my hair loss ultimately led to a successful business, embracing my baldness with pride was an important step in my life. I'm still not 100 per cent confident with the loss, but everyday I grow in confidence.

> **Alopecia is an autoimmune condition where the immune system mistakenly attacks the hair follicles, causing hair loss on the scalp, face and other areas of the body. It can present in multiple family members, which suggests genetics play a part in this condition. It affects both men and women and often first appears in childhood.**

The versatility of Black hair

Emma Dabiri (she/her), writer and broadcaster

I mix my styles up all the time, but most often my hair is braided. I adore traditional Yoruba hairstyles, such as suku, and often think about the fact that these are ancient hairstyles designed centuries – or even millennia – ago, to showcase the beauty of our hair and our features. The fact that they are simultaneously traditional, cutting edge and futuristic-looking is a demonstration of Afrofuturism in praxis! I feel excited just thinking about it!

Locs connect us to our history

Sinai Fleary (she/her), founder and editor of *Jus' Jah* magazine

Having locs exudes so much vigour because they symbolise cultural links to our history as Black people. Locs are a symbol of African and Caribbean history. As a woman of Caribbean heritage, it is extremely important for me to acknowledge my roots, and having locs is one way in which I do this. They remind me that I am not alone, but part of a beautiful spiritual and cultural movement. I think about those who had locs before I was born, like the Mau Mau Warriors in Kenya, or the Rastafarians in Pinnacle, Jamaica. As a Rastafarian myself, my locs have an additional importance – they keep me spiritually balanced as they embody my divine connection with Jah (God). Having locs is therefore more than just wearing my hair naturally, it represents my devotion and commitment to my faith and way of life.

My hair

Personally, my hair journey has been chaotic. By the time I was allowed to do my own hair I was truly doing the most. I wanted to look like one of the girls on the Just For Me relaxer box, but no matter how I tried, no matter how much heat I used to get what I perceived as a sleek, 'neat' look, all I ended up doing was burning my hair and it 'snap, crackled and popped', leaving broken hairs all over my bathroom sink. It was only when I learnt to moisturise my hair using the LCO technique. Liquid followed by Cream and sealed with an Oil – and realised that water was a friend to Black hair, not a foe, did my relationship with my hair improve.

I started to really embrace my texture and wear styles that didn't require so much work or manipulation. Now, I'll throw on a wig, slick my hair back into a ballerina bun or have a cute swoop fringe. But, I could decide to have Beyoncé blonde hair today, or an Angela Davies 'fro tomorrow. How I style my hair is a personal choice, and not a refelction of my abilities. It doesn't mean I am less capable, less professional, or that I lack intelligence. My hair doesn't define who I am. It doesn't dictate how I should be treated. It definitely doesn't need to be policed. It shoudn't make me more palatable or acceptable either.

Your hair

Black hair is so versatile and unique. You can go from a silk press to a kinky 'fro just by getting your hair wet. It shrinks and it can be stretched. It grows up and out. It can hold a style without pins, hair bands or clips. There's variation in our hair.

There's creativity in it too. One day, you might want to do a protective style, the next, it's a slicked back ponytail – then, you are doing up knotless braids and before you know it you're reaching for the peroxide just so you can have a little change. Your hair and the way you choose to cover it also tells a story – it might be about your culture, religious and political beliefs or your mental, emotional and physical well-being. **It's your hair. So it's your choice.**

Despite the constraints and campaigns that try to make us feel that our hair makes us somehow inferior, Black women have always used our hair to express our identity, individuality and personality, and also as a means of self-preservation, through the intricate designs in braiding that helped us to survive slavery. Think of the pioneering work of beauty culturalist and mogul Madame C.J. Walker. Through the development of Walker's Wonderful Hair Grower and the 'Walker System', she created scalp care products, shampoos, lotions and a hot comb that promised to give Black women's hair a 'beautiful silky sheen', and in doing so she became the self-made pioneer of a billion-dollar industry. Then think of the finger waves popularised in the 1920s, and later the big afros of the 1960s and 1970s that told everyone from miles away that we were **'black and proud'**. The Jheri curls of the 1980s that had our parents doing up Brazilian water wave way before you could get your bundles from AliExpress. Or the intricate gelled hairstyles of the 1990s that let everyone know you were an original bad gyal. There isn't just one style or only one look for us. Whether its headwraps, beads, wigs, extensions, weaves or your natural hair – anything goes. We continue to buck trends. We set them by wearing styles that inspire an entire generation. Whether it's Baby hairs. Kankelon ponytails. 'Mini buns' aka bantu knots. Bejewelled fringes. Or a simple middle parting.

So, when I see Black women embracing their look, I'm forever gassed.

Curlture's hair mantras

Jay-Ann Lopez and Trina Charles (she/her), the UK's leading natural hair influencers

There's no such thing as good hair

Your hair texture is perfect, don't let the world tell you it's better or 'less than' because it behaves differently. Coils, kinks, curls are equal in beauty.

You don't need to have straight hair

Your texture is beautiful as it is. The 'swish flick' feeling shouldn't change how you feel about *you*. Switch it up whenever you feel like, but don't forget you're magical as you are.

Health before length

Healthy hair is happy hair. Keep investing time into maintaining healthy hair, rather than worrying about different styles.

You do not need (long) hair to be 'feminine'

Having long hair (or having hair at all) doesn't make you more or less feminine. Your femininity is yours to define.

Unlearn the generational curses

'Nappy', 'picky', 'tough' are words that have been used to put down Black hair and you may hear them from family or friends. It's OK to disagree with them. Your hair is yours, and it's beautifully made.

Hair inspiration

★ Halima Aden wearing her hijab as she slays a runway show

★ An Instagram stylist that has you wondering 'What lace?'

★ Nicki Minaj wearing 30 flowing inches of Malaysian hair

✱ Letitia Wright's cropped look

★ Brandy's signature box braids

✱ Mel B's bantu knots

★ Michaela Coel, Liv Little, Paula Akpan, Ruth Sutoyé and Nicole Crentisil doing up supermodel with their Bald Black Girl agenda

✱ An aunty in her best church wig

★ Naomi Campbell's middle parting

★ Issa Rae giving us look after look in every single scene of a twenty-minute episode of Insecure

★ A Bad B with the biggest afro puff

★ Zadie Smith's headwraps

★ Ciara wearing canerows on the red carpet

★ Beyoncé's signature blonde locks in Fulani braids, kinky, curly ponytail, sleek and straight, or wet and wavy

Grace Jones's height-defying high top

★ Michelle Obama rocking kinky curly hair as soon as she left the White House

★ Lil' Kim inventing colourful wigs. Who else would have been brave and bold enough to have hair highlighter yellow?

★ Chloe and Halle's locs

★ A babygirl wearing bobbles and beads in their hair

So, big up all the magician hair stylists who can melt your frontal with precision and can attach box braids to less than an inch of hair. The babygirls who do hair, work full time and study. You truly are doing the Lord's work.

There is so much to say about hair. We are barely scratching the surface. But use this as something to refer back to as you continue on your hair journey. For some people it's just hair, but for you as a Black girl I understand just how important and expensive (!) it can be.

Below I have provided hair resources for you to help you on your journey.

BOOKS

★ **Hair Story**
by Ayana D. Byrd & Lori L. Tharps

★ **Don't Touch My Hair**
by Emma Dabiri

★ **Kink**
by Curlture

★ **Good Hair**
by Charlotte Mensah

★ **My Hair**
by Hannah Lee

★ **My Hair is a Garden**
by Cozbi A. Cabrera

★ **Palette**
by Funmi Fetto

★ **'Is your hair still political?'**
Essay by Audre Lorde

DO YOUR GOOGLES

★ Madame C.J. Walker
★ Annie Malone
★ Dr Afiya Mbilishaka

SONGS

★ **'I Am Not My Hair'**
by India Arie

★ **'Afro Puffs'**
by The Lady of Rage

★ **'Don't Touch My Hair'**
by Solange

FILMS

- ★ Nappily Ever After
- ★ Self Made
- ★ Back to Natural
- ★ Braided
- ★ Hair Love
- ★ Bad Hair
- ★ Pelo Malo
- ★ Hair that Moves
- ★ Pick

WEBSITES

- ★ Afrocenchix
- ★ Antidote Street
- ★ Brown Beauty Talk
- ★ Byooti
- ★ Psychohairapy

PEOPLE TO FOLLOW ON SOCIAL MEDIA

- ★ Curlture
- ★ Jaynelle Nicole
- ★ Joanne Kinuthia
- ★ Nikki Nelms
- ★ Funmi Fetto
- ★ Freddie Harrel
- ★ Nia the Light
- ★ Fesa Nu

BLACK OWNED BRANDS FOUNDED BY BLACK BRITISH WOMEN

- ★ Afrocenchix
- ★ Almocado
- ★ Anita Grant
- ★ Big Hair + Beauty
- ★ Bouclème
- ★ Charlotte Mensah
- ★ Dizziak
- ★ Equi Botanics
- ★ Flora & Curl

Squad goals

**How friendship and sisterhood
can shape your life**

By Melissa

You may call them your squad, clique, gang, crew or your people dem. Whether there's a whole group of you rolling deep or it's just you and your girl vs the world, your friends play an important part in shaping the person you are now and the person you are becoming. It could be as simple as helping you choose an outfit for carnival or as deep as giving you advice you didn't want but needed to hear – having your friends' support is invaluable.

'A lot of women, when they're young, feel they have very good friends, and find later on that friendship is complicated. It's easy to be friends when everyone's eighteen.'
Zadie Smith [1]

Natalie and I have gone through so much together over the years: bad boyfriends, even worse hairstyles, terrible outfits, problems at work and our first major girls' trip. Our friendship is built on being there for one another and always having each other's backs – whether I'm phoning her in the middle of the night or she's sending me ten-minute-long voice notes. I call her my **ride or die**, and she proclaims to everyone who will listen that she's my babyfather. No matter what or who we come up against, it's always **us against the world**. Our friendship has helped define who we are as women.

Although I like to think that I'm a force all by myself, when I get together with my girls **we are an entire movement**. We become unstoppable. I start to believe I can achieve anything. They empower me to reach my goals and deal with situations that are getting me down. That's how I know **Black Girl Magic** is real – it's the only way I can describe what it feels like to be surrounded by people who want to see you win. I wouldn't even be able to call myself grown if I didn't acknowledge the love and support that has helped shape the woman I am, and the woman I'm still becoming.

'Is solace anywhere more comforting than that in the arms of a sister?'
Alice Walker [2]

The relationships I have built with **people who look like me** can probably be singled out as the most definitive and life-affirming experiences I've ever had. People who grew up like me. Who spoke the same language I did. Who experienced the same things I did. It may seem minor, but for me, being able to just exist without having to explain the very essence of who I am is **kind of a big deal**. Being able to rant and rave without needing to break down why I feel what I feel is refreshing. I don't want to have to explain why I wear a silk scarf to bed. Or set out the pressures and responsibilities of being the eldest daughter in an immigrant family before I can complain about my parents. I shouldn't have to justify why I'm cancelling plans because it's a deep conditioning day, or why I'm hiding from the woman I just called 'aunty'. (No, I'm not related to her and, yes, my mum did tell me not to eat at her house.)

Natalie and I, for example. We met at secondary school.

There is something extra special in having those **people who just 'get you'**. Friends you can flash your eyes at and they're able to interpret exactly what you mean without any words. You know that look you give your girls when it's about to **go down**? That smirk you share when a plan is coming together? Or the way you all burst out laughing over an inside joke that doesn't make sense to anyone else?

These are the people who form part of my sisterhood. The family I chose. Girls I can cry with. Girls I share my deepest, darkest secrets with. Girls I party with. Girls I holiday with. Girls who give me great advice. Girls my parents absolutely adore.

But, sis, let me tell you something. I may have talked up how amazing my girlfriends are, but sometimes they are a real pain. So no, I'm not going to tell you that you won't remember arguments you had ten years from now because that isn't true! Believe me. Natalie still complains that I lost her first copy of *The Color Purple*, despite the fact that I definitely gave it back to her. It's been nearly twenty years!

You did not give it back!

Secondly, I'm **Pettyana**. I remember every injustice I have ever faced, whether it's my sister taking my make-up or Natalie eating my last chicken wing. Girl, I'm petty enough to remember my secondary school nemesis to this very day.

I don't want to make it seem like making friends is easy. You can't just shout, 'gang gang' and expect to conjure up three fully formed Insta baddies in matching outfits, who are willing to invite you into their squad, 'ayyy' with you on your stories and live happily ever after. **Relationships take work**, whether they are romantic, platonic or familial. To make sure they endure and grow with you, it's really important that you take time to nurture them – whether it's a friend you've just made or one you've known from day dot. Building friendships is like laying your edges, finding the perfect outfit for prom or studying for exams: you have to put the work in. Putting in minimal effort means getting minimal results. Minimal results equals **not living your best life**. And ain't nobody got time for that.

I found my squad when I found myself, using the same tips I'm going to share with you in this chapter. As you turn the pages, you may start to make connections with your own friends or situations you've experienced. I'm sure I won't be the first to tell you that as much as friendships can build you up, they can also tear you down. My mama always used to say, 'Show me your friends and I'll show you your future'. So, I want to **spill the tea**. I'll tell you all about the things that really matter when you're making friends, and show you how to strengthen those bonds.

'There's nothing like a conversation with a woman that understands you. I grow so much from those conversations.' **Beyoncé** [3]

I don't have a ready-made friendship group!

First things first. It is important that we acknowledge that not everyone has a close knit group of friends that they can rely on. For some of you, it may be that you just haven't found your people yet, or maybe you find it really hard to make friends or like spending lots of time by yourself. Don't worry, that's perfectly OK.

I'm incredibly lucky to be able to say that I finally have a network of incredible people in my social circle – people who I can firmly say form part of my sisterhood. But it wasn't always this way. I didn't always have my tribe, or feel like I was part of a girl gang. **Sure, I had people to chill with and, yeah, we could laugh and joke together. But to get deep?** I was too worried about being judged. I didn't feel safe confiding in them. To make it worse, sometimes we would argue. **Big bust-ups.** What was a simple misunderstanding could very easily become a cussing match. The group would split. I would feel isolated. Sometimes some of the girls were closer to each other than they were to me, which made me feel left out. Don't let Instagram fool you – people can be part of a seemingly enviable friendship group, complete with matching outfits, but still feel alone.

I'm telling you about my experiences of friendship to reassure you. It doesn't matter if you have one girlfriend who holds it down for you in more ways than you can count, or a whole squad who have your back. **You will find your tribe.** Remember, life is a marathon not a sprint, and there's no need to put additional pressure on yourself. **Tek time.** Forget what all the movies tell you – you won't meet all of your life-long friends in school. It's perfectly normal if you don't meet the ones who stick until later in your life. I didn't meet my girl Ashley until university, and I feel like I've known her forever. It's like she's in my head: we always seem to be going through the same things, and we often buy the same clothes (even after all of these years, we're still surprised when we turn up at an event with the same bag!).

So what can I do to meet more people like me?

If you are struggling to find people you can connect with on a deeper level, one good way to meet them is to join an after-school club, or take up a hobby. Being in a new environment is a great way to break away from the rigid friendship groups at school. Taking control and choosing your friends, rather than being friendly with someone just because they are in your form, allows for **stronger connections**. I understand that this can be super daunting, but there are ways to make it easier. Firstly, the activity you choose doesn't have to be something you're already amazing at, it can simply be something that interests you, or that you would like to learn more about. The fact that you are brave enough to sign up at all is half the battle.

Secondly, it's good to remember that one of the main reasons people join groups and clubs is so they can mix with people who 'get' it and have similar interests. It's likely that many of the other people at the club have come alone too. They are in the same boat as you, and they are probably just as nervous. In fact, they are probably hoping someone will talk to them first! Be the person who initiates a conversation – if someone is standing on their own, go up to them and ask their name and why they've joined the club. Even if you just talk to one person, it will have been worth it. The likelihood is that you'll meet people that you **share common ground** with. Take Black Girls' Book Club, for example – the majority of members attend events by themselves, but before they know it they have made friends with the girls at their table, are taking pictures of each other and even arranging to meet up again. I've gone on holiday with girls I met at BGBC!

BGBC's Five New (Friendship) Rules

1 SHOOT YOUR SHOT

I met one of my BFFs, Nadine, on the very first day of secondary school. I was super shy and nervous about being in a new setting with new people, and the only person I recognised in my form class was someone who hadn't always been a good friend to me. I was worried that I would be alone. I couldn't see anyone who looked like me, which made me anxious. Then I saw Nadine. I looked at her and knew straight away that I wanted to get to know her. I tapped her on the shoulder and said, **'Do you want to be my friend?'**. That was it. It was probably the bravest thing I had ever done.

> *'I am deliberate and afraid of nothing.'*
> **Audre Lorde** [4]

Years later, I am still as close to her as ever, and we've made lots of other friends together and through one another. She is someone I can confide in and someone I can always trust to be honest with me. **At the time, it didn't occur to me how being brave enough to ask a simple question could pay off**. Imagine if I hadn't said anything to Nadine? I wouldn't have had lots of the friends I have now – I doubt I would have even met Natalie. And I doubt you would be here, reading *Grown*.

So, let's try something new. **I challenge you to a Shoot Your Shot challenge**. The next time you find yourself in a new setting, take the opportunity to speak to someone new and ask them a question – it can be anything from where they got their jacket, to what their favourite book or film is – or simply, 'Do you want to be my friend?'.

> *'Some say we are responsible for those we love. Others know we are responsible for those who love us.'*
> **Nikki Giovanni** [5]

2 SHOW UP, SHOW OUT

You have to show up for those you say you care for, whether that means listening to your friend when they have an issue or helping them choose an outfit for a day out. **Be there for them.** There have been times that a friend checking in on me or sending me a meme has completely changed the course of my day for the better. Knowing that someone is thinking about you and wants the best for you makes you feel valued, important and loved. So make sure you do the same for your friends. **Gas. Them. Up.**

List five things below that you love about one of your BFFs.

1. ....
....

2. ....
....

3. ....
....

4. ....
....

5. ....
....

Now, tell them! Remember, people don't know how you feel unless you communicate. Make sure they know why they are such a good friend and just how important they are to you.

3 PUT IN WORK

Sometimes, you think you know your BFF better than they know themselves, which means you don't always remember to ask them how they are. I'm definitely guilty of this! That's why it's important to do a bit of **friendship maintenance**. By that I mean taking time to catch up in an intentional way (not just asking for gossip or planning your next outing). Thinking that everything is A-OK because your girl hasn't mentioned anything untoward, or assuming that they are having a good time just because you are, are the quickest ways for somebody's feelings to get hurt. As a friend, it's your responsibility to be aware of the little things that go unsaid.

Friendship maintenance is an integral part of preserving your relationships, so I want you to try something next time you feel like there is a bit of distance between you and your BFF. Ask to meet them at one of your favourite places. Then try the following:

Ask them how they are.
Are they quieter than usual? Do they seem unfocused or not themselves? Use this as an opportunity to show them that you are there for them. Let them know you have their back.

> '*You don't make progress by standing on the sidelines, whimpering and complaining. You make progress by implementing ideas.*'
> **Shirley Chisholm** [6]

Listen more than you speak.
This is my most important tip. No shade, but launching into a monologue about yourself shows a lack of consideration and can come across as pretty egotistical and self-centered. Listening more than you speak shows your friends that you are concerned and care about what they have to say.

Respond accordingly.
If they mention they are tired or run down, perhaps prepare a sleep-care package – hot chocolate sachets, a good book and a Spotify playlist that aids relaxation. If they are feeling anxious about an upcoming exam, send an encouraging text the night before to reassure them they're going to smash it. If they don't feel like speaking, then do something that will take their mind off their problems – send them a funny meme or a text listing five things you love about them.

These steps may seem basic, but sometimes we can be so wrapped up in ourselves that we forget to reach out. We have all asked someone how they are and then launched into a conversation all about ourselves. Or asked someone if they are OK, but not actually expected them to say anything other than, 'Yes'. It happens, so don't beat yourself up about it. We all make mistakes, it's how we choose to fix them that matters.

hello

4 KNOW YOUR BOUNDARIES

It's important that we understand and accept that **people aren't perfect**. Being human means that people will make mistakes and upset you, but you have to figure out whether you're willing to go through those ups and downs with them. That's when boundaries come into play. Deciding what I was willing to forgive and what aspects of friendship were non-negotiables not only changed my perspective, it made me happier too. Being able to identify things that trigger you, and putting reasonable steps in place to mitigate any issues with friends allows you to get one step closer to being grown.

Growing up, if someone treated me in a way I didn't like I would just **ghost** them. I would be so angry that I'd rather be petty than take the time to talk to them about how their behaviour made me feel. That was all well and good

hi

until I stopped speaking to a very good friend. When I calmed down, I realised that she was probably one of the only people who really **had my back,** but by then she had disappeared. Literally fallen off the face of the Earth. Sis, I was hurt! I was so caught up being Pettyana that when I calmed down and thought things through properly, I knew the argument wasn't worth losing a friend over – but it was too late. Now I know that I should have told her that her behaviour was pushing me away, and given her a chance to explain herself or make a change. She might not have even realised that she was upsetting me. Even after having had that conversation I had made a decision to end the friendship anyway, she definitely deserved more than me voiding the relationship we had built.

Have I upset you

Are you ignoring me?

hi

Try outlining your friendship boundaries below.

What you need in a friendship (your non-negotiables):

hi

....

....

What you like in a friendship (things you'd like to have, but it isn't a deal-breaker if you don't have):

....

....

What you don't like in a friendship (your deal-breakers):

....

....

Sis?

If you know your boundaries, it's easier to decide if a friend has **crossed the line**. This not only sets an indicator of what you won't accept in a friendship, but it shows what you are willing to do for a friend too.

Here's another piece of advice, and this one is really important: next time you have a tiff with a friend, don't ghost them like I did. Instead, try this exercise. Just before you go to bed, write down all the things that upset you and explain how they made you feel. In the morning, read through your notes. Do you feel any better? Do you still feel as strongly as you did before?

When you're feeling up to it, meet up with your friend and **explain how their behaviour made you feel**, and how it's impacting your relationship. Remember, you may have both tested each other's boundaries, so make sure you **listen to them too**. By following these tips, you're showing that you value your friendship, are ready to acknowledge that you're both upset, and are taking the time to rectify any issues without letting pride get in the way.

hi

5 SPILL THE TEA

It's good to talk. Good friendships are built by sharing parts of yourself. That may be through sharing secrets, revealing your goals, or even just asking for advice. By trusting friends with your innermost thoughts, you establish bonds that last for a lifetime.

> *'An envious heart makes a treacherous ear.'*
> **Zora Neale Hurston** [7]

Spilling the tea won't work with every person you meet. Some people will break your confidence, or judge you for something you have said. Sometimes, someone you trust may even start a rumour about you, or tell lies. It hurts. It can break your confidence and make you think twice about sharing personal information. Unfortunately, there are no tips for avoiding that. Some people are just badmind, and there's nothing you can do or say to change them. All you can do is practise discernment when it comes to choosing your friends, set boundaries and hold your head high.

> *'Who gon' check me boo?'*
> **Shereé Whitfield** [8]

I tend to only share my deepest secrets with people who have the same ideals and values as me. It means that I don't feel judged. **Sometimes, secrets can feel like a burden.** It can be a lot of pressure having to carry your own secrets or even those of the ones you love. Knowing something that no one else knows can make you feel alone, like no one understands what you're going through. But having someone you can trust and confide in allows you to alleviate any feelings of embarrassment and shame around a secret. It allows you to discuss a difficult situation, work through your feelings and perhaps find a solution.

> *If someone asks you to keep a secret that you don't feel comfortable keeping, it is OK to tell a trusted person. This could be your doctor, guardian, teacher or even an anonymous helpline. Share the load.*

Check yourself

Friendship is a two-way street, and sometimes you have to take a step back and reflect on your own behaviour as a friend. It's your responsibility to ensure that you're treating your friends with the same dignity and respect you expect from them. It might not always be pretty – self-reflection often reveals things about yourself that you might not like. Sometimes, we are out here screaming 'Bun badmind' or 'No bad vibes', not realising that WE are the ones bringing the **bad vibes.** But that's what being grown is about: knowing when you've stepped over the line. **Check yourself before you wreck yourself.**

1. Don't take things so personally

Sis, not everything is about you. Don't let your ego control your emotions and have you out here taking offence at people just living their lives. At times, we can be hypersensitive about things that others had no idea would even impact us. Don't overreact. If you know that certain things trigger you, tell your friends and set those boundaries. This may sound like tough love, but your real friends won't try to intentionally upset or hurt you. If your BFFs' actions make you feel bad, it's important that you are honest with them and don't keep those feelings bottled up. Doing so can lead to resentment and create fractures in your relationships.

2. Don't expect too much of your friends

Our friends are not our therapists. Yes, a good friend will be there for you, but please don't always rely on your friends to make you feel better about yourself or change your mood. Being the friend that is constantly giving advice or is being leaned on can be incredibly draining and causes an imbalance in your relationship. Remember, a healthy friendship is a balanced friendship.

3. Ditch the drama

This is self-explanatory. Sometimes we bring passa passa to our own door. Stay out of people's business. If it doesn't affect you, guess what? It doesn't concern you. No one likes a gossip or being around someone who can't hold water. If you stay out of other people's business, that means you have more time to mind your own.

4. Don't rely on others for validation

Babygirl, you are enough. You're more than what people expect of you. You're bigger than your wildest dreams. You don't need anyone, including your friends, to validate who you are or why you are there. Take up space, sis.

The importance of sisterhood

Dorothy Koomson author

I've learnt the hard way that sisterhood begins with yourself. I used to be all about indiscriminately supporting other women – particularly Black women – in whatever they try to do. I used to be all about unthinkingly having another woman's back in whatever battle they were engaged in. But, time and time again, I found that when it came to me needing someone to have my back – my back was bare. Eventually, I learnt to look before leaping to the defence of someone else, and to think about whether I'm strong enough to support that person. Am I being my own best friend, my own supportive, loving sister whenever I do something for another woman? Sometimes, the answer is no, sometimes the answer is yes. But always the answer should include, 'I am honouring the sisterhood by taking care of myself first'. That means it's important to help when you can, to take care of yourself when you can't, and to always approach the world in a hopeful, honest manner.

Make your own rules

This chapter isn't the definitive guide to friendship – these are just things I have learnt that work for me. We want to inspire you to be grown, so take what you want from these pages and make your own rules. Remember, friendships can change and develop over time. You can't predict who will always be there for you and who will have your back. All you can do is put the work in and ensure you value and nurture the friendships you have.

Reclaiming your time

Part 1

Real talk: Dealing with microaggressions

By Natalie

always remember attending ballet classes at my school when I was seven years old. I was the only Black girl in my class. I was so excited to go to lessons and used to carry my ballerina bag to school with pride – but this didn't last long.

'I feel most colored when I am thrown against a sharp white background.'
Zora Neale Hurston [1]

I was never given attention during the class or the encouragement other students received. I wasn't given any help to learn the routines. I was never selected for main roles in the performances. And, **no matter how hard I tried**, I was always in the back row for each and every class. I remember feeling upset and asking my mum why it was happening. She mentioned something about my teacher having 'favourites' and that I wasn't one of them. Shortly after this, my mum took me out of the class.

This incident was the first time I felt I was being treated differently for no real reason. My ballet teacher would always comment that she didn't know how she was going to teach girls with 'such heavy bones', or she'd talk about how big some of us were (when actually I was so skinny at the time my mum had taken me to the doctor to check I was healthy) and how much 'grace' we lacked. As a child, I didn't realise that my teacher was referring to the theory that Black people have denser bones and was implying that it was harder for her to teach me ballet because I was Black.

Now, I look back at that situation and understand that my teacher was discriminating against me. She had bought into many of the stereotypes about Black people and the belief that there was no role for us in classical pursuits. **I may not have exactly understood her nonsense at the time, but I still felt hurt by her actions.** My mum felt it too. The last straw was when she noticed that not one of the girls of colour in my class had been selected to represent our school at the annual competition that we had all worked so hard towards. To her, it was obvious that I was never going to get the teaching I deserved, and she could see that being treated badly in the class was beginning to damage my confidence. I didn't know until recently that my mum had been so furious that she even brought my aunty to watch me during one of my classes. She didn't tell my aunty her suspicions about my teacher beforehand, but at the end of the class she asked her what she thought. My aunty told my mum she thought the teacher was racist. When I talked to my mum about this nearly twenty-five years later, she remembers it like it was yesterday and still gets angry. More importantly, **I still remember it, I still get upset and I still feel angry about it**.

I am sharing this story because sometimes things happen to us as young girls that make us feel ostracised, simply because we are Black. **We know it is wrong,** even if at the time we can't put our finger on exactly what is being done to make us feel the way we do. I am here to let you know that it isn't all in your head. My mum didn't tell me explicitly that she thought my teacher was discriminating against me because I was Black – it went unsaid between us – but I understood why I was no longer going to be in that class. I don't remember asking my mum why I couldn't go back to that class or asking if I could stay.

I wish I could say that this was just a random event and that my ballet teacher was a bad egg, but throughout my girlhood I experienced this treatment in so many different ways. I witnessed my friends suffer the same treatment and even saw them being punished at school when they stood up for themselves. Calling out racism could get you in more trouble than the person who was actually being racist, especially if that person was a teacher. Usually **I felt like I couldn't speak out** about the racial discrimination I suffered and that I saw other Black girls around me suffer – and, even if I did, nothing would be done because I couldn't prove something was racist.

I am not the only Black girl who has gone through this – you may have been made to feel the exact same way. It might not have been a ballet class for you, maybe it was at an after-school club, such as gymnastics or football. It could have been someone following you around in a store, suspiciously watching your every move while white customers were left to shop freely, or something a friend said to you about Black people that was meant to be funny. It could have been a stereotypical comment about your hair or your body that made you feel uncomfortable. Maybe it was someone mispronouncing your name, or giving you an English one that was 'easier' for them to pronounce. These are all examples of 'othering' – experiences that make you feel excluded or outside of the 'norm'. I was lucky that my mum understood what was happening to me at my ballet class and was able to remove me from the situation, but many Black girls aren't able to leave situations that make them feel othered so easily. Maybe they don't know how to explain what they're feeling, or don't have someone in their corner they can talk to.

In this chapter, I am going to have these conversations. I am here to tell you that your feelings are valid, that these moments are real and that you don't need to be able to prove it. Here, I will help you figure out how to process and communicate those feelings and ensure that you are respected at all times. You are valued and you don't have to accept disrespect.

Racism is defined as 'the inability or refusal to recognise the rights, needs, dignity or value of people of particular races or geographical origins. More widely, the devaluation of various traits of character or intelligence as 'typical' of particular peoples.'

Oxford English Dictionary

|2|

Racism and microaggressions

Racism comes in many forms, and often it appears to be covert or innocent. **There is no form of 'innocent' or 'unconscious' racism**, and whether it is obvious or undercover, it is still racism. Someone doesn't have to say the N-word, make direct comments about Black people or be physically violent to be racist.

A shop assistant who only follows Black customers around would probably say they weren't racist and that they were only doing it because, in their experience, the majority of the people who stole from the shop were Black. But this shop assistant is racist. They are buying into **harmful stereotypes** that are perpetuated and used against Black people to control, bully and silence them. These events can make us feel uncomfortable, hurt and insecure. Words, statements, questions and behaviours like those of my ballet teacher are **microaggressions**.

Microaggressions are usually small, negative, judgmental slights or insults. They can be throwaway jokes (at a Black person's expense) or comments that make rude assumptions about Black people. For example, someone could assume you are a good singer or good at sports just because you are Black, or expect you to know about where they went on their safari because you told them you are from Nigeria. A microaggression could be someone asking you where you are 'really' from, assuming you weren't born in this country because you are Black, or don't match their narrow idea of what a British person looks like. Sometimes, it can be your teacher always overlooking your contributions, or your classmates not valuing your input. People making you feel like what you have to say isn't important because the ideas and contributions of Black women are so often undervalued or not given the credit they deserve. A common microaggression is the assumption that you are 'ghetto' or 'street' simply because you are Black, or the expectation that you know about everything 'urban', regardless of where you live or how you have grown up. (More about this from Mel in the second part of this chapter.)

> A *microaggression* is defined as 'a statement, action, or incident regarded as an instance of indirect, subtle or unintentional discrimination against members of a marginalised group such as a racial or ethnic minority.'
> **Oxford English Dictionary**
> [3]

Microaggressions aren't about you as a person, they are about minimising and dehumanising you in a backhanded way. **That's why they can be so stressful.** Sometimes, it isn't clear whether you are just being sensitive, or whether the person made the comment with a bad intention. Either way, if something makes you feel excluded, you have the right to challenge it.

I didn't understand what a microaggression was until I had left university and started working, but once I found the term, I was relieved. Finally, **I had the language to discuss things** that frustrated me, things I couldn't previously explain without someone telling me that it 'wasn't racist'. We should not be so quick to excuse microaggressions – don't feel pressure to use any higgy hagga analysis or critical reasoning to try and justify someone else's actions because you don't want to accept the fact that they are racist. If you have to go around the houses to say it's not racist, it probably is.

BIG FACT

When someone says, 'You're not like other Black people', this isn't a compliment. This person is saying that you are more acceptable than the stereotypical Black person. That is offensive. That comment is based on negative perceptions and can make you ashamed of your Blackness, even if it was framed as a positive observation.

> **BIG FACT**
> Indirect or small incidents can cause just as much hurt and stress as a being called the N-word or suffering overt racism. Don't let anyone make you feel like you don't need to take smaller incidents seriously or speak out about them. If it made you feel a way, it made you feel a way and you don't need to tolerate it.

White fragility

A lot of the time, when we call out racism and discrimination, we are made to feel like we are the ones at fault. Many people are not ready to accept that they are racist or are products of a racist society. Many white people can be defensive or feel uncomfortable when we talk about racial injustice and this is **white fragility**.

If you call out racism, do not back down because that person is offended. They should be looking to understand their own behaviour and apologise. Don't feel like you can't call out those closest to you (even your family members) for being racist either, or assume they can't be racist simply because they show you love and care about you. Your own family can love you and still make you feel excluded because of the colour of your skin.

We often fear calling out discrimination because we don't want to suffer the repercussions of calling someone racist, or have our complaints dismissed or ignored. Growing up, I saw so many people get punished for calling teachers racist when those teachers had been discriminating against Black students. Nobody wanted to hear it or investigate what had happened. The teacher's word was the truth – even if there had been witnesses who agreed that the teacher's actions were wrong. When you see this time after time, knowing all the things that could go wrong if you try to explain how you feel, it can seem easier not to speak up at all.

Say it with your chest

We all need the room to talk about times we have felt uncomfortable, excluded or othered, and Mel and I are here to speak on it with louding voices! So, feel free to offload in these pages about your own experiences – **say it with YOUR CHEST, sis**.

Have you ever been made to feel excluded because of the colour of your skin?

....
....
....
....
....
....
....

How did the experience make you feel?

....
....
....
....
....
....
....

Is there anything you wish you'd said or done in that moment?

....

....

....

....

....

What will you do if this happens again?

....

....

....

....

....

R.E.S.P.E.C.T.

Respect is the basic, entry-level requirement of all social interactions, and it's what you should expect from everyone. You shouldn't simply adjust your expectation when someone is devaluing you because of the colour of your skin. There is nothing worse than simply grinning and bearing discrimination. **We have to show people how to treat us and we have to learn how to set boundaries.** It took me a long time to learn how to speak my truth, and to be clear with those around me about what is and isn't acceptable. This is something I still struggle with today when working in the corporate world, and it is something I continue to work on as I navigate white-dominated spaces. Respect isn't about never being told what you need to be told; it is about being treated fairly, and spoken to in a way which does not mock, belittle or degrade you.

Stand up, speak up

I know it isn't going to be easy to stand up for yourself – especially if you are the only Black girl in the group, or if the person who is discriminating against you is an adult or in a position of power. You may be fearful that you will be excluded from your friendship group, or belittled by a superior, but we are here to help you figure out the best way to speak up. We want you to feel confident when setting boundaries with those around you. Here are a few keys for dealing with microaggressions.

> *'People feel that if a racist attack has not occurred, or the word 'n*****' has not been uttered, an action can't be racist.'*
> **Reni Eddo-Lodge** [3]

1 Figure it out

Sometimes, you might not be able to tell whether something is outright racist, a microaggression or simply a bad joke. But try not to automatically think about someone's motivation or whether they're a 'good person'. Your focus should be on **how their action impacts you**. Does it make you feel uncomfortable or excluded because of your race? If it does, it's not OK.

It is always good to reflect on whether you are being oversensitive, but even if you are, it is OK for you to set boundaries with others. Be clear about whether certain jokes or comments are acceptable to you, and those around you should respect that.

If you need to take time to think through what has happened, take that time. Sometimes, we don't give ourselves the space to process the behaviour of others; it is normal to still feel upset about something days after it has taken place. Remember, this isn't something you need to be 'strong' about. The purpose of a microaggression is to make you feel uncomfortable, and you shouldn't just expect to get over it.

2 Write it out

If you don't know how to speak about what is happening, sometimes it's easier to put pen to paper to help you process it. Writing things down will also help you clearly explain the sequence of events. If you want to work through something that has happened that felt like a microaggression, use the space below.

....

....

....

....

....

....

....

3 Talk it out

Coping with racism and microaggressions is draining and stressful. **Do not suffer in silence.** Talk to someone about what is going on and how it's making you feel. This might be your best friend, your mum, your aunty or maybe a favourite teacher. Make sure you only confide in people you trust and feel comfortable with. Don't allow anyone to dismiss your feelings.

Remember that not everyone will understand what you are going through. I remember facing racism at work and the person I confided in (who was older than me and Black) tried to convince me that I was mistaken – even other Black people may not always understand.

If you have suffered trauma, you may need to speak to a therapist. Do not be afraid to ask for the help you need if talking to those around you just isn't enough.

4 Take action

If you are now in a place where you want action to be taken, take the time to think about how you want to deal with the incident. Sometimes, you just want acknowledgment that what happened was wrong and to get an apology. Or you may feel it is right for the person to be removed from their position or punished. Either way, **it is your choice** to pursue the avenues available to you to ensure someone is reprimanded for their racist behaviour.

Once you have identified what you want the outcome to be, identify who you need to speak to. If you want an apology, you may go straight to the person who discriminated against you. If you feel it is necessary, you can explain to them why their actions or words are not acceptable in order to facilitate an open conversation that ends with you getting the apology and the recompense you are entitled to. Please make sure you have this conversation in a space where you feel safe. You might even want a friend or someone you trust to be present too.

You may not want to have a one-to-one conversation with the person whose racist behaviour has caused you trauma, and that's understandable. You may want to have a conversation with a mutual friend, teacher, parent or someone else you trust who can then speak to the person on your behalf and ask them to apologise.

If you think the person needs to be held professionally accountable for their behaviour (for example, if a teacher has made a racist remark in the classroom, or a shop assistant has refused to assist you), you may want to make a formal complaint. You shouldn't be intimidated by a formal complaint process no matter how long and drawn out it may seem – **it is your right to make your grievance heard**.

It takes courage to take a stand. I cannot promise you that every time you talk about what you have faced, people will actually listen. Sometimes you may decide it is better to soldier on rather than escalate it further. The bottom line is: it is your experience so it is your choice. Do whatever you feel is right for you.

5 Walk away

We do not need to fight and stand up to racists every time we encounter them – sometimes the best option, like in my ballet class, is to **remove ourselves from a situation** that is not good for us. Only you know what you can truly stand. Your mental wellbeing is important and it is OK to take yourself out of a toxic and damaging environment. If you are in a situation where you are being bullied or discriminated against, and there is a route out which won't disadvantage you in the long run, please take it.

Don't feel like you need to stay around people who make racist remarks or ostracise you because you are Black. If your 'friends' continue to make jokes about Blackness or consistently make you feel uncomfortable, even after you've told them that it isn't acceptable, they are not your friends. You may not feel strong enough to call them out on their behaviour, but you don't have to stick around and keep experiencing it. You deserve better for yourself and from those you call your squad.

Don't be shy

Chanté Joseph (she/her), journalist, writer and social media creative

Don't shy away from speaking about what you know is right, even if the world around you says otherwise. You can form great bonds and connections with people online who share your beliefs, and on the days when it feels like too much remember there are many more people fighting with you and for you! Social media can be a scary and intimidating space but it is important to curate your feed; follow people that inspire, motivate and educate you. Use your accounts as tools to do more of what you love.

Expectation vs. reality

Just because someone is nice to you and seems to like you, it doesn't mean they always have your best interests at heart, or that they won't limit your potential. I can't sugar coat this for you because it's a serious issue: sometimes people will take an interest in you and make you feel like they have your back, but they can still hold damaging stereotypes about Black people. It could be your best friend, your favourite teacher or your love interest.

When I was in sixth form, I applied to an introduction programme for future law students at the University of Cambridge. I was so excited. I knew I wanted to do a law degree, and now I would get a chance to spend a week seeing what it would be like to study at one of the best universities in the world. So, I took the letter to the head of my sixth form. But he told me there was no point in me applying and that it was 'a waste of time'. I trusted him – he had interviewed me and given me the offer to join the sixth form – so if he was telling me the opportunity wouldn't count for much, I wasn't going to go. When I look back on this moment now, though, I feel so disappointed that I missed out. I've now accepted that my teacher just didn't really see me as the type of student who should be going to Cambridge.

This wasn't the first time I'd had to deal with other people's low expectations of me. I always felt I had a point to prove. I was one of the only Black girls in the best school in my borough, and I knew that many of the students I studied with didn't think I belonged there. At the beginning of my second year of sixth form, I was told that I needed to sit right at the front of my politics class. I knew my classmates assumed I'd been moved because I was a bad student, and I started to believe that too.

The good thing about sitting at the front of the class, though, was that I could see all the notes my teacher had made about students on the register. Anyone who knows me knows I have eagle eyes, **I don't miss a trick**. So, after I accepted my new seat in the class, I looked at the register and saw I had achieved the highest grade in the class for my politics A level. Everyone else on my table also had high grades. That's why I was at the front – it was because I was good! But everyone had expected me to underachieve. They believed I wasn't as capable as the other students because I was Black and because I spoke a certain way, and sometimes that is hard to accept.

You have nothing to prove

I was so angry about being harshly judged that I focused a lot of my energy on proving everyone wrong by working harder. Now I have learnt that I never had a thing to prove to anyone, and neither do you. Sometimes your very presence in an all-white space will be a problem for others who don't think you should be there, but this isn't your issue to take on.

We are often taught that when someone discriminates against us, it is our job to show them that their low expectations are wrong. No. It isn't your job to prove to others that the stereotypes about Black women aren't true. **You shouldn't need to work twice as hard for half as much as your white peers.** Please do not internalise the pressure to be perfect – racism and discrimination cannot simply be 'outworked', the same way that being from a privileged background or coming top of your class will not shield you from microaggressions.

Focus on living your best Black life. Be who you are, continue to do the best you can do. You have nothing to prove. People may be unnecessarily harder on you because of the colour of your skin – all I can tell you is to be aware of it, talk about it with those you can trust, and most importantly KEEP DOING YOU.

Take the time to look after your mental health

The pain caused by racial discrimination doesn't just float away into the atmosphere. I know we are told to be strong, but that doesn't mean you have to put racial trauma to the back of your mind and keep it pushing. You can be traumatised just by seeing how other Black people around the world are being treated. When I see Black people suffer from discrimination, police brutality, receiving poor medical treatment and facing obstacles simply because of the colour of their skin – the same skin I have – it impacts me. I can't witness Black suffering and function as normal simply because it didn't happen to me. I feel connected to those people because we share a mutual identity. Make sure you talk about your feelings and express how these events are impacting you.

It's OK to be tired

Dealing with microaggressions and racial discrimination is tiring. Even as a grown woman, I sometimes just want to live my life without having to worry about what white people assume about me before I have even opened my mouth. You may feel the same. You might just want to be a babygirl and enjoy a carefree life. None of us wants the pressure of having to always interpret the real meaning behind what someone has said. It is exhausting feeling like you don't belong in certain spaces or like you always have to defend yourself.

It is not your job to explain to people what it's like to be Black. Sometimes people will want you to set out bad expeirences so they can understand where you're coming from, but these conversations can be triggering. The fact is, racism is real; Black people have been discriminated against for centuries. It isn't new and you shouldn't have to explain or re-live trauma in order to educate a person who should take the time to educate themselves.

'We must love each other and support each other.
We have nothing to lose but our chains.'
Assata Shakur [5]

Be the voice you want to hear

Chelsea Kwakye (she/her), author

At age seventeen, no one tells you how to feel when microaggressions no longer feel 'micro'. No one tells you how to overcome the emotions when one ignorant comment stays on your mind for days. For young Black girls, racial microaggressions become part of our everyday life, even to the point where you start to doubt your most trusted relationship – the one you have with yourself. But how do you get over this when being young and going to school means you naturally care about what people think and how they react to you? The key is learning how to draw boundaries and pick your battles. Part of that lesson is recognising that self-care can be, and should be, a radical act which forces you to actively put yourself before and above situations. Whether that's confronting friends, teachers or even family – be the voice you would want to hear during a tricky situation!

Never waste your time

Shamadean Reid (she/her), founder of WAH Nails and Beautystack

It's very easy to be othered, to be made to feel like an outsider, or that you don't belong. But what if you flipped that feeling on its head? What if you are precisely where you're meant to be, and everyone else is abnormal? Never waste your time and energy on spaces where you cannot feel at home. Be yourself – it's all anyone ever wants from you.

So how do we harness our power?

When we suffer discrimination or see others suffer it, we have a choice to make about how we deal with it. Not all of us have to be activists. It is about doing what you feel comfortable with: your lane could be protesting, donating money to anti-racist charities, speaking out about the discrimination you've suffered, raising awareness on social media, or creating opportunities for other Black people. Or, it could be simply taking the time to educate yourself about Black history and the impact of racism around the world – what we have been taught in school often conveniently leaves out the true horrors of slavery and colonialism (when European powers invaded or took control of other countries). It is important to know our history when it comes to tackling racism, and to be aware of the part that Western governments still play in suppressing our economic and political power.

It might take you a bit of time to develop the confidence you need, and to figure out how best to step into your power. Everyone has their own way of raising awareness. At the 2020 US Open, for example, tennis player Naomi Osaka wore masks bearing the names of victims of police brutality, including Breonna Taylor, George Floyd and Trayvon Martin. By wearing these masks, she kept the conversation going about the injustice of their deaths and kept the Black Lives Matter movement in the spotlight. She didn't listen when people told her to stop getting involved with 'politics' and just focus on sports, because she believed that it was her purpose in that moment to honour those victims and draw attention to racism. Doing so didn't stop her winning the tournament and taking home her prize money, either.

'I feel like I'm a vessel at this point, in order to spread awareness.'
Naomi Osaka [6]

Raising awareness and **challenging racist behaviours** is difficult, and people will question you. Even your friends may tell you you're being too 'political', but it is your right to work towards dismantling inequality that impacts you and other Black people around you. Many white people want to derail conversations we need to have about race. For example, when people assert that Black Lives Matter and the response is that 'All Lives Matter'. We can be made to feel we like we are being divisive but never forget that you are justified in fighting for equality. Protesting against racism is not easy. It takes continuous courage and resilience, because change doesn't happen overnight.

Finding your lane

As you learn more about racism and have more experiences, you may feel empowered to become engaged in active protest. At other times you may want to focus your energy on something else which you feel will enable you to contribute more to the movement at a later time. We are all moved in different ways when we see or experience racial discrimination, and below are a few questions you can ask yourself when trying to process your emotions:

What changes would you like to see in the world?

....
....
....
....

What skills/strengths do you have that you could use to help make those changes?

....
....
....
....

So, where does this leave us?

*'Being Black, especially a Black woman,
is a political statement in this country.'*

Natasha [7]

My experiences with racism and microaggressions have built me into the grown woman I am today, but they don't define me. I can't tell you how taxing it can be to be the only Black face in a room of white people, whether it's at school, university or at work. I can't promise you it will be easy to adapt when microaggressions and discrimination chip away at you daily, but what I can encourage you to do is have the strength to speak out, set boundaries and make it clear that you aren't one to play with. The failure of others to see you, your beauty, your value and your humanity is not something you should ever have to tolerate. Never let these things dampen your shine or hinder your progress, you are here for a very good reason - always remember that.

If you want to continue to educate yourself on racism, microaggressions and how to deal with them, here are some books I can recommend:

And here are some brilliant anti-racist organisations to look up:

* **The Hate U Give**
  by Angie Thomas

* **Noughts and Crosses**
  by Malorie Blackman

* **Dear Martin**
  by Nic Stone

* **Why I Am No Longer Talking to White People About Race**
  by Reni Eddo-Lodge

* **This is Why I Resist**
  by Dr Shola Mos-Shogbamimu

* **Living While Black**
  by Guilaine Kinouani

* **No White Saviours**
* **Black Lives Matter**
* **All Black Lives UK**

I rise

Faridah Àbíké-Íyímídé
author

Maya Angelou once said, 'I rise, I rise, I rise', in her famous poem 'Still I Rise'. This poem – as well as many of her poems, and much like this message I write here – is a love letter to Black girls everywhere. It is a self-love anthem, telling us that when the world does not see us, when people tell us we aren't enough or that we are too much, we are magical enough to rise. It's hard to believe that sometimes – that you are magical, especially when so many people tell you that you aren't. But you are. Trust me.

When you look in the mirror and you see your beautiful afro and your amazing dark skin, know that you are enough. You always have been, and you always will be. Using the words of Maya's love letters to all the Black girls in the world, look at your reflection and tell that girl, 'I am enough, I am beautiful, I am magical, and I rise, I rise, I rise.'

Part 2

Defining yourself: Understanding sterotypes

By Melissa

Remember when we discussed Professor Kimberlé Crenshaw's theory of intersectionality in Chapter 1. Well, there's a principle that sits alongside it – and that's **misogynoir**. Misogynoir is derived from the Ancient Greek words *misein* (to hate) and *gynē* (woman), which together form the modern-day English word 'misogyny' (prejudice against women), and the French *word for black, noir*. The word misogynoir was coined by feminist writer Dr Moya Bailey and was later developed and popularised by Trudy, creator of Gradient Lair, a poignant blog written by and for Black women. It is used to describe the different forms of particularly nasty anti-Blackness and sexism that Black women face. It also highlights the cultural perceptions and social identity of Black women, recognising that we aren't able to separate one from the other.

'What happens to Black women in public space isn't about them being any woman of color. It is particular and has to do with the ways that anti-Blackness and misogyny combine to malign Black women in our world.'

Dr Moya Bailey [8]

Discovering the word misogynoir was a huge lightbulb moment for me after years of not only hearing about, but also facing, different microaggressions. Knowing there was a term that explained my experiences and that of other Black women was almost a comfort. **I wasn't alone.**

There was often something more insidious and underhand about those experiences that was hard to pinpoint or articulate. I knew exactly what was happening. The same thing was happening to all of my friends. My own mother would tell me about her experiences at work as she cooked our dinner in the evening. But I didn't yet have the vocabulary to articulate how the discrimination that I faced was fundamentally different to that experienced by friends with different racial or gender identities to me. Looking back, from a very young age I knew that some of the treatment I faced was about more

'[The Black woman] had nothing to fall back on: not maleness, not whiteness, not ladyhood, not anything. And out of the profound desolation of her reality she may very well have invented herself.'
Toni Morrison [9]

than just being Black, but **I would constantly second guess myself**. I would even end up gaslighting myself. (Gaslighting is when someone manipulates another person into questioning their own thoughts, memories and beliefs.)

As a Black girl, this experience may become a normal part of day-to-day life for you. And I'm not going to lie to you – not much has changed. I've just gone from discussing with my friends which teacher had 'tried it' with us during break in the school yard, to calling Natalie in the loos at work to make sure I'm not overreacting to a colleague's snide comments.

But now I am empowered. And that's because, thanks to Dr Bailey and Trudy, I understand what misogynoir is and know that those who engage in it are seeking to devalue and discriminate against me. It's not because of anything I've said or done – it's because of their prejudice and ignorance. I see it coming a mile away. But even when I don't, I no longer beat myself up about it. Understanding what this behaviour is means I'm no longer rendered defenceless. Knowledge is power, and

'We must reject not only the stereotypes that others hold of us, but also the stereotypes that we hold of ourselves.'
Shirley Chisholm [10]

I am enlightened. I'm better equipped to deal with the emotional ramifications of the trauma these interactions may bring, and I'm actively able to shut down and challenge discourse that seeks to diminish who I am. Now, I pity anyone that attempts to pit me against my peers. Or seeks to use tired tropes and stereotypes to oppress me. **I can advocate for myself as well as support and uplift my sisters.**

This part of the chapter is going to get real. Real quick. As much as this book is about empowerment and loving the skin you're in, I wouldn't be your big sis if I didn't spill the tea and talk about the subjects that may make you feel uncomfortable. I acknowledge that you may read some things that upset you. Perhaps because **it finally makes sense**. You may recognise some stereotypes. You may be familiar with some of the behaviour. Other things you will never experience a day in your life. But that doesn't mean they don't happen. If it's not you, it may be one of your friends. Use this chapter to help and support them. Let them know that they aren't alone.

It's important that we speak about what it's really like growing up as a Black girl. The good, the bad and the ugly. Some may say you should wait until you're older to break down the realities of racism, but what good does that do when you're already going through it? If you can experience it, you can learn about it, and it's my mission that once you really peep game you will feel empowered enough to reject those stereotypes.

What does misogynoir look like?

★ Black girls being excluded from school at a proportionately higher rate than their white peers.

★ Black girls being accused of being aggressive, loud or challenging authority when they ask questions in school or advocate for themselves.

★ Black girls being seen as needing less protection because it is assumed they can defend themselves.

★ Black girls not being taken seriously when they complain of feeling unwell or ill.

★ Black girls being deemed 'ghetto' for hairstyles and fashion that are celebrated when worn by their white peers.

★ Black girls minding their own business in shops but being watched by security guards who assume they're going to steal.

★ Black girls being stereotyped as sexually advanced, grown or 'fast', meaning when they report allegations of abuse, they are ignored.

★ Black girls receiving less support with schoolwork than their peers as it's assumed they won't do well anyway.

★ Black girls being penalised for failing to conform to Western beauty standards if they choose to wear their hair in natural styles.

★ Black girls being made to take pregnancy tests by medical professionals despite not being sexually active.

★ Black girls not being comforted or provided with support during difficult times.

★ Black girls being more harshly punished than other children as they are perceived to be more mature.

★ Black girls having to explain that someone they are playing with is their sibling and not their child.

★ Black girls being hypersexualised before they even reach puberty.

These examples are just some of the ways in which we as Black girls and women are discriminated against in our everyday lives. **This specific combination of anti-Blackness and misogyny criminalises Black girlhood, while abusing and destroying Black Girl Joy.**

#IWANTYOUTOSEEME

Nyome Nicholas-Williams (she/her),
a self- and body-love advocate, plus-sized model
and mental health activist, speaking here to
Kayela 'Lala Love' Damaze

I struggled growing up and being comfortable in my body. I had an
eating disorder from the age of fifteen until I was nineteen. I always found
it difficult to accept that I was a tall and broad girl, and tried to control it by
barely eating which led to me picking up disordered eating. I grew to learn
that my height was powerful and that my worth has never been, and never
will be, defined by my weight.

Now, as a model and activist, I focus on the liberation of fat
Black girls – and pushing for change in the type of bodies
used in the media and in fashion. It is so important for
Black women to be brought back to the centre of 'body
positivity'.

Some of the biggest misconceptions about being fat
are that I am lazy, that I am lying about being happy
in my own body and that I couldn't possibly be happy
and be fat. These are concepts that so many people
struggle to grasp. It's important to take time in
accepting yourself and your body. There is no rush,
but you need to show yourself compassion and you
can't be hard on yourself. Self-love will come, it
just takes time and growth!

Stereotyping

This behaviour is usually influenced by negative stereotypes that people hold about Black women – preconceived ideas about what we're like and what we do. This could be that we're too angry, too 'ghetto' or too grown, even if there is no corroborating evidence. These stereotypes are socially constructed, which means they have been created based on assumptions and then been widely accepted by lots of people. Their purpose is to put Black women down and justify others' bad treatment of us. These stereotypes can impact your own view of yourself, making you feel compelled to change and adjust your behaviour in order to appease others. Known as assimilation, this can force you to change the way you look, the clothes you wear, how you behave or even how you speak, just to ensure that you fit society's standards of what is 'right' and 'proper'.

American academic Patricia Hill Collins defines the way that stereotypes are used to shape Black girlhood as 'controlling images'. Put simply, these negative images help to justify the discrimination and bias we experience. So, lets discuss some of the social stereotypes about Black women and girls.

'Stereotypes provide social scripts for how people are expected to view and treat Black women. More importantly, they are the social scripts that Black women are expected to internalise.'
Patricia Hill Collins [11]

The Angry Black Woman

The Angry Black Woman trope was probably the first one I was exposed to. From a very young age, I instinctively knew that by virtue of what I looked like, I would be perceived as more aggressive than my white friends. There's no mistaking it.

To be deemed an Angry Black Woman is to be painted as irrational, hysterical, aggressive and unreasonable when you try to assert your opinion or advocate for yourself. This tactic is used to stop you dead in your tracks. To make you feel ashamed for speaking up for yourself. To make you feel that your reaction to a situation is incorrect or 'too much'. Sometimes, in the moment, you don't know whether to keep vocalising your point, or switch to proving that their assessment of your character is wrong. It's a **catch-22**: either you stop defending yourself almost instantly, or you actually end up getting angry because of the injustice. This allows the perpetrator to feel smug in the knowledge that no matter how you react, they will be proved right.

Calling us Angry Black Women is a quick and easy way for others to deflect from whatever issue we're raising. When something or someone is deemed as unreasonable or hysterical, it becomes easier to dismiss and ignore. What was a valid concern or response to poor treatment is now seen as the ranting of an irrational, hypersensitive Black woman. This is an attack on our characters and it belittles us. But, remember, this stereotype is meant to control us. They want us to change our behaviour so it's more acceptable to them – more submissive.

As hard as it may seem, it's important that you don't internalise these messages. You don't need to adapt your behaviour and you definitely don't have to make excuses or justify your actions if you are angry. **Remember: your thoughts and feelings are always valid.**

'I'm always annoyed about why Black people have to bear the brunt of everybody else's contempt. If we are not totally understanding and smiling, suddenly we're demons.'
Toni Morrison [12]

Uses of anger

Kelechi Okafor (she/her), podcaster, writer and actress

There are numerous examples of the ways Black women have been locked into the Angry Black Woman trope. For a long time, I too believed that the way to get free of this was to show myself to be exceptional, because we are told as young Black girls that we have to work twice as hard to get half as much. The truth that I found, and many other women need to find, is that this alone is not enough.

Considering all the historical and present-day travesties inflicted on marginalised and underrepresented groups – from the enslavement of Black women that led to being raped and brutalized, to the non-consensual experiments carried out on Black women's bodies in the name of science – we have a right to be angry. The anger is what we need to break free. Respectability politics won't save Black woman. In fact, respectability politics won't save any woman. I believe that anger is one of the things that can.

Live your truth

Kayela 'LaLa Love' Damaze (she/her), wardrobe stylist, fashion and lifestyle influencer, and model

You don't have change who you are to fit society's unrealistic standards. Live your truth, and remember that your Blackness is allowed to be unapologetically magical.

The Grown Black Girl

Writing this is difficult. As big sis I want to be able to preserve your innocence, but I also want to help prepare you for the actualities of what you may experience by virtue of being a Black girl. This topic is tough. It means bringing up and thinking about things that are often seen as taboo. This might even be something that your parents or guardians don't have the correct language to discuss with you – they may even ask to revisit it at a later stage. If you want to, you could ask them to read this section first, or to read it along with you. Giving you the opportunity to safely discuss the topic with those who love and care for you is incredibly important. If you're not ready to read this, that's OK. This section will be here for you when you need it. *Grown* is your companion, assisting you as you grow up and navigate the everyday realities of life. **So, let's get into it. Who is the Grown Black Girl?**

Before I understood what it all meant, I personally couldn't wait to be grown. Grown to me meant dyeing my hair, getting acrylic nails and a pedicure. Having a boyfriend and buying myself clothes. Going to the club and doing brunch with my friends. But in reality, it's more than that.

You may have heard the phrases 'too grown', 'fast' or 'force ripe pickney' before. They are simplistic, gender-specific terms aimed at young Black girls to indicate that they are intentionally behaving in a sexually provocative manner. I guess it's a slightly kinder and more sanitised version of calling them a 'ho' or 'sket', but essentially these words are used to hypersexualise Black girls.

'I felt betrayed by my body because it dared to bloom.'
Nicole Dennis-Benn [43]

Hypersexualisation refers to the way in which society imposes sexual meaning on a person's body or their actions. Have you ever been asked if you can twerk before someone bothers to ask your name? Have you ever been referred to as 'caramel' or 'chocolate'? These are examples of the ways in which people sexually objectify Black girls – **reducing who you are to nothing more than your body** and what it looks like or what they think it can do.

The hypersexualisation of Black girls is nothing new, from the depictions of Sarah Baartman in the 1800s to the images of Beyonce today. Black childhood is meant to be a pivotal point in our lives. It's a transitionary period where we are learning what it means to be *us*. Where we learn to be grown. But if sexual language is directed at us when we are on the brink of adulthood, it immediately takes away our innocence. We often do not get to access the privileges of girlhood, such as being able to be naïve, innocent or to make mistakes in the same way our white counterparts do. Often the whole 'coming of age' experience just doesn't seem to exist for us. We are forced to move from childhood to adulthood in such a fast and brutal fashion that it seems like one afternoon you're in your living room bussin' a wine in your house clothes, and the next you are being told to dress 'respectfully' and that your shorts aren't appropriate in mixed company.

When those inside and outside of our community suddenly declare that you are 'no longer a little girl', you can go through myriad emotions. On one hand, these people are recognising your maturity, but on the other they are prematurely stripping you of the protection afforded to little girls growing up. How often have you been expected to look after your younger siblings despite there only being a few years age difference between you? Or wash plate while your brother plays? Perhaps you felt uncomfortable around a particular uncle, but your family put your behaviour down to rudeness? You might even have major family responsibilities, such as being the main translator for you parents, having to inform them of life-changing decisions or break bad news to them. All this pressure without anyone considering that an eleven-year-old should be playing games, not calling the council. **Being grown comes at a cost.**

This is where **adultification** comes in. Adultification is when Black girls are perceived as being louder or stronger or more sexually advanced and experienced than our peers, and we are treated badly for it. Unfortunately, this is something I know only too well. I remember an incident in primary school where my class had been invited to the local community hall to watch a visiting South African choir with our families. I was so excited, and I couldn't wait to go. I had even taken the time to plan my perfect outfit – a co-ord crop top and leggings with dalmatian print. (It was the 1990s, so don't get too mad at me!) I barely remember the concert, but I will never forget what happened the next day at lunch break. Laura M – a white girl from another form – marched over to me. She declared at the top of her voice, 'My mum saw you at the concert yesterday and she said you're a little tart. You're always showing off.'

I couldn't have been more than eight or nine. But I was already being perceived as grown. My body was being viewed through a sexual lens before I even knew my times tables. I was just a babygirl, I didn't have boobs and I hadn't even started my period (not that it would have mattered if I had). At that age, I had already watched enough *EastEnders* to know that being called a tart wasn't in reference to a sweet treat.

Looking back, being deemed as fast and being sexualised by an adult at that age is outrageous. It's dehumanising. Where my parents saw their daughter dressed in a cute, fashionable style, Laura M's mother saw me as – for lack of a better word – a 'ho'. She had painted me as an attention seeker and a seductress – a sexually promiscuous woman, showing off her body for the attention of men. And in doing so, she stripped me of protection and transformed me from an eight-year-old girl who still sucked her thumb and played with Barbie dolls to a big woman with sexual experience. I wasn't even a teenager, let alone a consenting adult.

At the time, I remember being quite stunned. I don't remember responding. I didn't even tell a teacher. I wasn't upset – I was embarrassed. In my young mind, Laura M wasn't as intelligent as me. She wasn't allowed to choose her own clothes like I was. She wasn't praised or picked for special school projects like me. She was always being written up in the 'bad behaviour' book and getting told off by her mum, and I often avoided playing with her. So I just brushed it off. I was one of few Black girls at the school, which already meant I was different. I put her behaviour down to my basic understanding of racism. I decided her comment was unjustifiable and that she was jealous of me. I ended up pitying her. She had a nasty mum, just like the characters I'd read about in Roald Dahl books – the ones that used bad language and were as ugly on the inside as they were on the outside. So I moved on and I forgot about the incident. But I didn't forget how that comment made me feel.

Unfortunately, that wouldn't be my last experience of the Grown Black Girl stereotype. I recall playing with my little sister in the paddling pool when I was ten years old. My next-door neighbour saw me through the garden fence and told me I was 'too grown' for that. It was in that moment I noticed my changing body. I remember quickly wrapping my arms around myself, covering my chest and quickly finding a towel so she could no longer see me. Ultimately, she made me feel like I had done something wrong. My dad, however, was furious when I told him, and immediately went to B&Q to buy materials to build a new fence (lol). The fence he built was taller this time – sturdy enough to keep her from peeking in. But that didn't stop the secret from getting out. I was growing. My body was changing. The damage was done.

As I grew older and my body changed, I experienced cat calls and street harassment. I started having to think twice about the clothes I wore, sometimes going up a size or two to avoid comments on my body. Often, it wasn't even words – it's the stares. One look can have you feeling ashamed and vulnerable. As Nicole Dennis-Benn so eloquently put it, it's like our bodies are working against us.

The Grown Black Girl stereotype forces us to see our bodies in ways that we probably aren't even ready to. Not only that, it ensures that we are constantly kept hypervigilant. It's like every element of Black girlhood is policed, from our hair to our bodies to what we choose to wear. **Hypersexualisation means we're perceived as little women before we even get to see ourselves as young girls.**

The Loud Ghetto Black Girl

'Ghetto', 'ratchet', 'loud', 'facety', 'sassy', 'unrefined', 'unpolished' and 'unfiltered' are all stereotypical characteristics that dehumanise and punish Black girls who do not fit society's expectations of so-called appropriate behaviour.

The Loud Ghetto Black Girl is criticised for her patois-inflected speech and told to speak 'properly'. She plays her music loudly at the back of the bus, screaming "Ayyyyy!" as she gasses up her friends. She's the girl with the voluptuous lips, shiny and sticky from 99p hair shop lip gloss, who slides into the Lil' Kim squat as soon as a camera is pulled out. To me, she's **just a carefree Black girl**. I was that Black girl. I still am.

Black girls are defined as too angry. Too loud. Too aggressive. They are seen as tongue-popping and neck-rolling. Big gold hoop earrings and name plate necklaces. Acrylic nails and long eyelashes. Caricatures with colourful 30-inch weaves. When we are judged on looks, we are treated as inferior, and bad behaviour aimed towards us becomes justified.

The Loud Ghetto Black Girl trope is a harmful amalgamation of all the ugly stereotypes placed on Black women and girls. **These labels seek to reduce the Black girl experience to nothing more than a one-dimensional character.** When we are labelled as 'ghetto' it determines how much respect, protection and support we deserve. Not only this, it takes away from our self-defined personhood, regulating us to unfeeling, vacuous creatures. Non-human talking heads who don't think or feel, and are simply around to serve as the punchline to a joke. This trope fails to recognise the complexity of our Blackness and diminishes our own individual identities.

'To be "loud" is to demand to be heard. To have an "attitude" is to reject a doctrine of invisibility and maltreatment ... To be a ghetto Black girl, then, is to reinvent what it means to be Black, poor, and female.'

Monique
W. Morris [131]

And yet, with a tongue pop here and a neck roll there, others appropriate interpretations of Blackness like an ill-fitting coat. Black girls are repeatedly marginalised by a society that mocks their speech and way of dressing. That is, of course, until a more palatable face claims ownership of our trends, making them sanitised and consumer-friendly. Black girls are being shadow-banned on TikTok for the way they look, while their peers are blackfishing or posting videos, speaking in forced patois or African-American vernacular – a 'blaccent' – stringing random words together for comedic effect.

Ghetto until proven fashionable

Shakaila Forbes-Bell (she/her), fashion psychologist

Drip, swag, style. Whatever you want to call it, self-expression through aesthetics has always been a crucial part of the Black experience. Black people spend a higher percentage of their income per capita on hair, beauty and clothing than other racial and social groups. Not only has this pattern existed in several countries, it's persisted since the early 1990s. From a psychological standpoint, the importance that Black people place on style speaks to a desire to celebrate our culture and history, which is so often devalued in many areas of life. Your look is something you can control, an expression of your identity that is not as easily silenced, and yet, the restraints of Western civilisation have persisted in stripping African and Afro-diasporic styles of their richness.

The number of Black styles that have been watered down and repackaged for white audiences is laughable. A recent example comes from Sondreanna Huff, a Black Floridian woman who showcased pink eyelashes on social media only to be ridiculed and called 'ghetto' in her comments. Fast-forward to February 2020, when fashion magazine *Allure* featured coloured falsies as a hot new trend. From layered gold jewellery, to baby hairs, the Black aesthetic is a driving force behind global hair, beauty and clothing trends. The lingering remnants of slavery have caused our looks to be expropriated, appropriated and, as designer Nareasha Willis coined, 'ghetto until proven fashionable'.

Sadly, this anti-Blackness is so pervasive it's been subconsciously internalised by some people within the culture. Often, when luxury brands become accessible to the wider public, you'll see a few Black people jump to voice their annoyance that its 'become ghetto'. This negative response is internalised racism in action. When you subconsciously desire to be one of the 'good/different' ones, anything that celebrates Black culture will threaten your ability to fit into that Westernised mould. Simply put, these people haven't grappled with the fact that they're trying to fit into something that was never designed for them in the first place.

The Bad B

A short story. Five letters. One word. Simple, straight-to-the-point, yet highly effective. But when it's said, it's like a slap in the face. **It packs a punch.** It takes away your agency. It tells a story that you didn't ask anyone to write. It immediately strips you of your humanity. Your accomplishments no longer matter. You are no longer worthy of protection. You're no longer worthy of grace. You're no longer even you. You're reduced to nothing more than a capital B. Belligerent Black girl. Angry, sassy, grown, rude, fast, loud. A female dog.

'Irrepressible. She is insulted, but she holds up her head; she is scorned, but she proudly demands respect ... The most interesting girl of this country is the colored girl.'
Fannie Barrier Williams [115]

When the B word is thrown around it's typically used as an insult, a means of control. The B word puts Black girls in their place. It's meant to shut us up, sit us down and reduce us to nothing more than a stereotype. A teeth-kissing, side-eyeing, neck-rolling caricature of Black girlhood.

But what happens when bad actually means good? Growing up, I was really offended by the B word. It was rude and degrading. It made me feel less than, and was often a quick way for people to force me to change my approach when I was trying to get a point across. But when I really deep it, the word was only ever used to portray Black women and girls like myself as bitter, aggressive and unhappy. In reality, it was consistently aimed at girls who were nothing like that. Instead, **these were girls who were able to speak up and defend themselves.** Who wouldn't back down. Who couldn't be moved. Whose no meant no. Whose yes meant yes. These girls weren't pushovers and they weren't rude or aggressive. They were assertive. They had boundaries. They knew their rights. Ultimately, these girls were making themselves seen. These girls took matters into their own hands. They demanded respect, and if you didn't give it to them, they would take it.

Being a Bad B

Candice Carty-Williams
(she/her), author

Being a Bad B means knowing thyself and loving thyself. Even the bits you might think need work. Work on them and love them while you do.

From baddie Bey to bad gal Riri, **everyone wants to be a Bad B.** The 'Bad B' is the Black girl's response to being labelled as too fast, too angry, too much and not enough. The Bad B is what happens when we decide to fight back and reclaim words originally designed to control us. In her coming-of-age novel *The Coldest Winter*

Ever, the author Sister Souljah introduced me to what it meant to be a Bad B. The lead character, Winter Santiago, describes a Bad B as *a woman who handles her business without making it seem like business.* For me, being a Bad B is symbolic of independence. It symbolises strength. It symbolises confidence. She's a savage. She's classy. She's bougie. She's ratchet. There are no limitations on who she is and what she can be.

My grandmothers are my definition of the baddest to do it. Strong, Black women who were daring and didn't take rubbish from anyone. My mum's mum is small in stature and my Dad's mum was built like a brickhouse. Thick with two cs. But they were both formidable. Their fingers bejewelled with a collection of rings my grandfathers had bought them to express their love and adoration. They both taught me about freedom – the importance of a good education, the strength in having my own money, what it meant to be loyal and trustworthy and the benefits of being charming. They ensured I knew the path my ancestors had walked, taking time to tell me about my history and where I came from. But best of all, they taught me that I was enough.

So, when I think of Bad B's, I think of Bad Black women – and I mean that with the utmost respect. The B stands for boasy, beautiful, braggadocio, braggadocious, broughtupsy, brilliant and bold. She's unbossed and unbothered. I think of my family. I think of my grandmothers. My mother. My sister. My literary fairy god mother's - Sharmaine Lovegrove, Malorie Blackman, Dorothy Koomson, Nicole Dennis-Benn, Sara Collins, Toni Morrison, Maya Angelou, Zora Neale Hurston, and Leone Ross. Fictional characters who typified the glow up - Hilary Banks, Toni Child, Janie Crawford Killicks, Winter Santiago and Celie. Entertainers such as Spice, Lady Saw, Lil' Kim, Melanie Brown, Beyoncé, Kelis, Megan Thee Stallion, Louise Simone Bennett-Coverley aka Miss Lou. Sporting Legends like Serena and Venus Williams, Florence Delores Griffith Joyner, Shelly-Ann Fraser-Pryce, Veronica Campbell Brown, Merlene Ottey, Alia Shanee Atkinson. Iconic change-makers whose determination helped to pave a way: Nanny - Queen of the Maroons, Claudette Colvin, Shirley Chisholm, the Rt Hon Diane Abbot MP, Baroness Lawrence of Clarendon - Doreen Delceita Lawrence, Ruby Bridges, Asli Hassan Abade, Una Marian, Mae C. Jamison and Funmilayo Ran-some-Kuti. And Aunty June Sarpong OBE, who I think of everytime I wear glossy lips.

So, now when someone calls me a BLEEP, I just throw Bad in front of it. I say thank you, and take it as a compliment because it means I'm doing something right.

You decide who you are

Now, babygirl. I don't have all the tips to teach you how to 'deal' with these stereotypes and warped perceptions of who you are. I can't lie to you – they can be traumatic to experience. You can't help but internalise it. Right now, you may be thinking of a whole host of things you can do to prevent it. Wear the right clothes. Speak 'proper'. Adopt Westernised hairstyles. Try not to stand out. Be excellent. Sis, you do not need to take on the pressure of being a mascot for all Black people on your shoulders. I'm here to tell you that you it's not going to work. We can develop protective strategies such as code-switching – speaking formally or in English in front of your certain people, but reverting back to your mother tongue, patois or slang when you are with your family and friends – in order to take the power back and retain control of our identity. But, ultimately, changing who we are or attempting to assimilate won't work in the long run. It's a waste of time. Respectability politics isn't going to save you, sis.

So, what do I do? I practice Patricia Hill Collins method of 'self-definition'. This is the idea that you **hold the power** to dictate your own destiny (something I have been very vocal about throughout this book). Ultimately, I reject negative and imposed definitions of my Blackness. I surround myself with other Black women who seek to affirm me and see me beyond how I speak or what I wear. Surrounding myself with those who look like me and understand my experiences has allowed me to unlearn negative thought processes and love myself for who I am unconditionally. I uplift my friends. I am their cheerleader. I listen to their fears and support them with their dreams. I let them know that there is more to who they are than the projections of others, and that they always have a safe space with me. **I embrace all elements of who I am unapologetically.** I can be the angry, sassy, unrefined or uncultured Black girl and still be worthy of protection and respect. For me, self-definition is self-determination. I decide. I won't let anyone impose their negative perceptions of who they think I am on to me.

You might need to sit with this one, sis. There is no rush to be 'that girl'. It's a learning process and at my big big age I'm still doing the work. So, don't worry if you are finding the subject

'The emotional, sexual, and psychological stereotyping of females begins when the doctor says: "It's a girl".'
Shirley Chisholm [13]

overwhelming. Tek time. Think about it. Read books and articles on it. I have mentioned the work of Patricia Hill Collins, Professor Kimberlé Crenshaw, Trudy and Dr Moya Bailey in this chapter to start you off. There are also artists such as Lil' Kim, City Girls, Cardi B, Beyoncé, Ari Lennox, Summer Walker, Spice, Lady Saw and Megan Thee Stallion who have worked hard to reject society's expectations of them that are rooted in the way they look, dress or speak. Why not watch their interviews on YouTube to feel inspired? Finally, talk to people in your life who love and care for you and ensure you, are surrounded by those who embrace every inch of what makes you, *you*. For now, I'll leave you with this quote:

'Sometimes, I feel discriminated against, but it does not make me angry. It merely astonishes me. How can anyone deny themselves the pleasure of my company? It's beyond me.'

Zora Neale Hurston [17]

NON-FICTION

★ **Hood Feminism**
by Mikki Kendall

★ **Black Feminist Thought**
by Patricia Hill Collins

★ **Ain't I a Woman**
by bell hooks

★ **Bad Feminist**
Roxane Gay

★ **Eloquent Rage**
by Brittney Cooper

★ **Redefining Realness**
by Janet Mock

★ **Thick**
by Tressie McMillan Cottom

Sister Outsider
by Audre Lorde

FICTION

★ **The Bluest Eye**
by Toni Morrison

★ **Their Eyes Were Watching God**
by Zora Neale Hurston

★ **Namina Fornas**
by Namina Forna

★ **Mama Day**
by Gloria Naylor

★ **For Colored Girls Who Have Considered Suicide When the Rainbow is Enufe**
by Ntozake Shange

★ **Piecing Me Together**
by Renée Watson

★ **The Autobiography of My Mother**
by Jamaica Kincaid

6 Body language

Your body, your choice

By Melissa

Now, this chapter comes with a **slight trigger warning**. You may know by now that Natalie and I aren't going to shy away from any topics. This is *The Black Girls' Guide to Glowing Up*, of course, and we are always going to give you that realness. **And that's on period**. Whether it's boobs, batty or your lady bits, being able to have open and honest dialogue about your body is an important part of not just learning about how your body works, but also giving you the tools to love the skin that you are in.

Now, this trigger warning isn't in place because I don't think you are mature enough for the subject. It is more so to ensure you have adequate support as we discuss the ins and outs of that girlhood to womanhood transition, in detail. This is quite a sensitive topic, so you may wish to speak to a parent, guardian, older sibling or trusted friend before you jump right in. Remember, while *Grown* is always here for you, it's still really important that you **reach out to someone you trust** if do you have further questions.

While discussing sex in our community is often taboo, it doesn't stop people using terms such as 'grown', 'fast' and 'loose' to punish young women who are being themselves unapologetically and to justify abuse they may face. But, by shying away from important topics, we can end up increasing feelings of uneasiness and discomfort - leading to girls and women feeling that they are unable to voice concerns or speak up.

Trigger warning

If you are an adult reading this prior to sharing it with the babygirl in your life – please don't hide it from her! I know discussing sex can be uncomfortable and embarrassing. For a lot of us, it can feel like talking about sex at a young age is the first step towards having it. But let's keep it real. A lot of adults don't really know how their own bodies work, so realistically, how can we expect young girls to?

As a parent, you might be afraid to ask questions yourself, so you'd prefer to let girls figure it out themselves or learn about it at school. But remember, making natural and normal everyday occurrences taboo not only encourages embarrassment and shame, it also allows for spaces where the young ones in your life might listen to those who may not have their best interests at heart. Children form opinions about their body at a young age, and it is our responsibility to help them develop a positive body image as well as a good understanding of how their body works. This is especially important when you consider that the school curriculum does little to cater to the culture and experiences of those who fall outside of the mainstream.

So, now is definitely not the time to feel shy. We are discussing it all, from periods to punani. From boobs to bacterial vaginosis. Some of you might not even know what all of this is. But for those who do – yep, I'm really going there, sis. Ever wondered why your knickers end up bleached? Or why you have diarrhoea when you're on your period? Or why your parents started telling you to 'face your books' as soon as you hit puberty? Then this chapter will lay bare all the things you may have wondered but didn't know how to ask. We are ensuring that you have access to the correct information and the right support. Before you even really need it. *Grown* is our attempt to break generational curses and cycles, preventing all the babygirls from making the silly mistakes we did.

So, if you've got this far, I guess we can get right into it.

Going through changes

Earlier on in Chapter 5, I discussed ideas surrounding adultification and why being seen as 'grown' can be harmful for young girls. Well, often what is perceived as a 'grown' Black girl is simply a teenager going through puberty. Being labelled in this way is another example of how Black girls often don't get to enjoy their childhood in ways that are afforded to their peers. Changes to our bodies can sometimes lead to unwanted attention. Whether it's the double takes or family members remarking that you're a 'big girl now', changes in our bodies are a talking point before we even get a chance to become comfortable with them – or even to become aware of them ourselves.

So, what is puberty exactly? Puberty is essentially when your body begins to develop and change as you start to grow and mature. During this time, your body produces hormones that not only lead to physical changes, but can also affect how you feel emotionally. You may develop breasts, start your period and grow pubic hair. You may become taller. As your body starts to change, you may notice weight gain and see some changes to your body shape, such as your waist becoming more defined or your hips becoming slightly wider. It's not unusual to sweat more and you might start to get spots. You may start to have sexual thoughts and feelings or find that you are more irritable, upset or unsure of yourself than usual.

Girls generally begin puberty around eleven years old. But it is completely normal for puberty to begin earlier than this – it may even begin a lot later – and there is nothing to worry about if you notice changes at a different time than your friends. I was wearing a bra by the time I was nine, and started my period aged ten. While I was too embarrassed to let my school friends know, my mum had taken time to explain to me in private what to expect. If you notice that changes are starting to happen, do talk to a trusted caregiver and ask any questions you need to. Remember, you are not alone – **we've all been there!**

Tig ol' bitties

Boobs, breasts, tits, titties, melons, jugs, breasticles, bosoms, the twins, tig ol' bitties. Yours may even be blessed with cute nicknames - I personally call my left one Tia and the right Tamera.

From people on TV or music videos, to your favourite influences and Insta baddies, people will often talk about breasts as if they don't serve a biological function. Boobs - especially big bouncy ones - are seen as social currency. The prettier the girl, the bigger the boobs, the higher the likes.

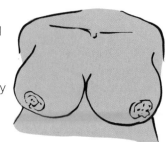

Often if you don't have those assets it can leave you feeling less desirable, feminine or grown. It can be a real hit to your self-esteem if you notice friends or people you admire have different boobs to you. But, despite what people say, your breasts are literally just two fleshy mounds on your chest, and having too much or not enough of that flesh doesn't define who you are.

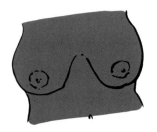

For many of us, having boobs was probably the first visual sign that were becoming grown. Getting your first bra was seen as a right-of-passage. It was right up there with your first kiss, getting your period, wearing make-up and getting your ears pierced. But no one tells you that **it's a process.** You know those growing pains people speak about? It doesn't just refer to the journey from girl to grown. It refers to the real pain that you may feel when your body starts to develop and grow. The hormones released during puberty causes the breast tissue to grow, and as it does, it stretches, which explains why you may feel some pain.

Now, I've got to let you in to a little secret. You may get those pains. It may really sting. But, after it all, you might not even end up with big boobs. I didn't. I was an A cup well into university. The thing about boobs is - just like your body - they vary from size to size and from person to person. Not only that, but your nipples and areola may vary too. Genetics play a big part of what your boobs look like, as does your weight and age.

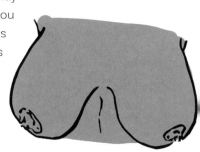

If your boobs are saggy, different sizes, set apart, set together, super perky or slightly droopy, shaped like a cone, a bell, teardrop or basketball, that's all perfectly normal.

Your areola may be dark. They may be light. Brown or beige. They may cover the majority of your boobs or just a bit of them. All of that is perfectly normal too. No matter what people say. Or lead you to believe. There isn't a typical look. All breasts, nipples and areola are distinctive and **unique.**

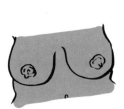

The only thing you must be mindful of is if the appearance changes. If your breasts don't look like how they usually do, if they are bruised, sore, producing discharge or if you notice any lumps, it's important you speak to your GP or a healthcare professional.

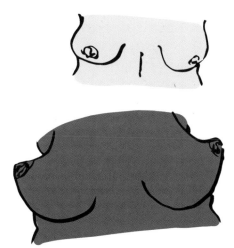

★ *Protruding nipples?*
Perfectly normal.

Flat nipples?
★ *That's normal too.*

★ *Bumpy nipples?*
An everyday occurrence.

★ *Puffy nipples?*
You may be on your period.

★ *Hairy nipples?*
You are not alone.

★ *Inverted nipples?*
Plenty of us have them.

★ *Third nipple?*
Very normal.

★ *Big nipples?*
There is no such thing as too big.

★ *Small nipples?*
No such thing as too small.

Vagina

From **foofoo** to fanny, there are lots of names we give to the situation going on between our legs. Regardless of what you choose to call it, the vagina is something that is rarely spoken about – leaving a lot of us wondering if everything is OK down there, or whether it looks 'normal'.

Most commonly, we refer to our private bits as the vagina – but its real name is the vulva. The **vagina** is actually just the opening. It's where blood comes out during your period and where you would insert tampons or a menstrual cup.

There's also the **mons pubis** or **pubic mound**, which is the triangle area in front of your pubic bone that will be covered in hair once you start puberty.

Just above your vaginal opening is your **urethra**, where your wee comes out.

There is also your **clitoris**. On the outside this looks slightly like a bean, and it's probably the one thing my mum didn't tell me about herself. I bring it up because it's important that we move away from viewing the female anatomy as taboo. Truthfully, the clitoris is often ignored when discussing sexual education for kids, probably because its function its purely for sexual pleasure. Now, you may be slightly too young to be thinking about all of that (or maybe you're already familiar with it), but getting to know and understand your body is not only a great way to encourage body positivity, it also quite empowering too! Understanding your body, what you like and what you don't, is really the beginning of understanding what consent is all about (more on this later). This allows you to have ownership over your own body and gives you the space to make decisions that you are comfortable with.

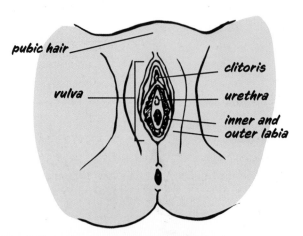

pubic hair

vulva

clitoris

urethra

inner and
outer labia

There are also your **inner and outer labia** – most people refer to them as your 'lips' – which can vary in size from person to person. Some of us have large prominent outer lips, some have prominent inner lips, some have asymmetrical inner lips, some have curved outer lips. You may have long, dangling inner or outer lips. You may have small open lips, or perhaps they are closed.

> Whatever the size and however it looks, there's no 'normal-looking' vulva.

I haven't forgotten **pubic hair**. I know it's random and can be embarrassing if you are the first one in your group of friends to get it. It may also seem useless, but it does have a function. Just like your eyelashes, it acts as a barrier – protecting the vagina from dirt and some bacteria. The arrival of pubic hair often signals the start of puberty and it keeps your foofoo warm.

So, now you're well-acquainted with you private parts, how can you look after them?

You should wash your private parts with **unscented products**. The vagina isn't meant to smell like a rose garden or your favourite Chanel perfume, so there isn't a need for special washes or wipes. These products are designed to play on your self-esteem, leading you to believe that you don't smell 'right'. In fact, heavily fragranced or perfumed soaps and body washes can upset your pH balance and might lead to bad bacteria, which can cause common vaginal infections such as thrush or bacterial vaginosis.

Thrush / yeast infection

Wearing tight, synthetic clothing and underwear can also lead to yeast infections. If you find that your bits are itchy or sore, your discharge changes from its usual colour or you have a noticeable smell, this could be evidence of an infection.

Bacterial vaginosis

This is another condition caused by bad bacteria multiplying in the vagina – your vaginal discharge may become grey and have a watery consistency with a strong, fishy smell. Remember, the more perfumed soaps and washes you use, the worse the problem will get.

Vaginal discharge

It's a sticky one, but yes, sis, I'm going there! As a former nurse, my mum was very open with me and always seemed quite comfortable when I asked questions about my body and sex and topics that some would consider 'grown'. She would often take time out to have important conversations with me – telling me about things before I got old enough to feel self-conscious or embarrassed and asking me questions to make sure I understood.

Despite that, though, in those early conversations we didn't ever discuss discharge. This meant I spent a lot of time thinking I wasn't normal. Sis, when I saw that random mucus-y fluid in my knickers I nearly had a heart attack. It basically looked like clear snot. First, I thought I was dying. Then, I kept telling my mum I had thrush and asking her to buy me medication. At one point I thought it might be an STI (Sexually Transmitted Infection) – even though at that point I had never even spoken to a boy let alone let one of them touch me! After months of embarrassment, I finally told my mum what was going on. She let me know that I wasn't alone, and it was **perfectly natural**.

My mum assured me that the clear discharge I was experiencing was simply the way the vagina cleans itself. She then explained that discharge is often thicker or more noticeable after a period – which explained why she had ensured she always bought me panty liners to use once my period ended. I was relieved. Knowing that discharge was perfectly normal and healthy took a big weight off my shoulders. Having a frank and honest conversation allowed me to feel comfortable enough to ask more questions about other subjects that were troubling me.

The mad thing about discharge is that it can actually cause that bleached stain that you may have seen in the crotch of some of your underwear. No one ever talks about it. But we all know about that 'dirty little secret'. Which isn't actually dirty at all – the discolouration is simply because your vaginal discharge is naturally acidic. This acidity helps to maintain the vagina's natural pH balance and prevent infections. You can wear panty liners to protect your underwear (more on this later). But if you don't feel like putting a panty liner in your pants all the time, then there are other things you can do.

What did it look like?
Was it itchy?
What colour was it?
Did it smell?

- Wear lighter coloured underwear that won't show your discharge stains.

- Rinse or wash your baggy immediately after taking them off (if you have Jamaican parents, you will probably already have been taught this).

- Spray the crotch with a stain remover and let it soak for a few hours before washing.

Remember, if your discharge isn't smelly and doesn't have an abnormal colour – such as yellow, green or brown – and doesn't have a thick or lumpy consistency similar to cottage cheese, then this is just a natural part of your vagina cleansing itself. Nothing to worry about!

Periods

The dot. Being on. Aunt Flo. TTOTM, or That Time Of The Month. Your monthly visitor. Girl problems. Whatever you choose to call it, menstruation – or your period – is the monthly bleeding that occurs when your body gets rid of the tissue it does not need. Put simply, the lining of your womb thickens as part of your monthly hormone cycle, preparing itself to support a potential pregnancy. The shedding and bleeding that follows during our period is what happens when a pregnancy does not occur. The entire menstrual cycle usually lasts between twenty-one and forty days, and periods usually last around two to seven days.

Every person's flow is different. Some people will have a heavy flow, while others will have a very light one. Or you might have one or two heavier days, but be very light for the rest of your period. You might even just get spotting – the odd drop of blood – for a few days. While a heavy period is normal, if it is too heavy, making you feel unwell or weak or really affecting your ability to go about your normal life, you may need to speak to your GP. There is help available if you need it.

It's impossible to predict how old you will be when your period starts, and there's no 'right' age. But, however old you are, you need to know what products you can use to help you feel as comfortable as possible.

Tampons

These are menstrual products that you insert into your vagina, where they expand as they soak up the blood. To remove it, just gently pull on the string that is left dangling on the outside, and out it comes! Tampons come in a range of sizes. FYI: the size of a tampon relates to how heavy your period is and how absorbent you need it to be. It's got nothing to do with how big your vagina is – having a 'wide-set vagina' is not a real thing, and a tampon is not going to stretch your fanny!

On day one of your period you may need a super-sized tampon, but by day seven you may only need a light absorbency one, or even just a panty liner. Tampons can be used for roughly four to six hours. If you decide to use a tampon, I recommend trying a regular size first – this will help you figure out whether you need to go up or down a size depending on what works best for your flow. If you find removing a tampon feels dry or uncomfortable, then you will need to go down a size. If you find it's leaking or filling up a lot sooner, then you will need to go up a size.

Leaking is a **normal** part of learning to manage your period, and, as you figure out what works for you, you will find that you become more attuned to changing your sanitary products before an accident happens. But remember, even if you aren't leaking, that doesn't mean your tampon can just chill in your foofoo. Leaving a tampon in for too long can lead to infections, or even **life-threatening conditions** such as toxic shock syndrome. So, if you notice an unpleasant smell, a change in your vaginal discharge, you start to get a fever, experience vomiting, dizziness or are suffering from pelvic pain, it's important that you remove your tampon quickly and seek medical advice.

Tampons can be a great choice – they allow you the **freedom** to go about your day-to-day life without having to change your plans. They're brilliant if you want to do active things like go swimming or visit the gym as they aren't bulky and won't budge when you move.

> **P.S. Your tampon can't get lost inside you!** It stays where it is until it's pulled out – the fact is, there is only so far up it can go. However, if it is left in for too long, it may become compressed making it difficult to remove, or the string may end up inside you too. You may need to do an extra manoeuvre, but eventually you should be able to feel for the tampon itself and pull it out. Now, don't be shy – this is your body and it's the only one you've got, so you shouldn't be afraid or scared of it!

Sanitary towels, or pads

Probably the most straightforward product is the sanitary towel because it is used externally. You just stick the pad to your knickers and keep it moving. They are a good option when you have your first period as they are convenient and easy to use. No missing strings here! Sanitary towels come in a range of absorbency sizes and shapes, with higher absorbency pads created especially for night-time use.

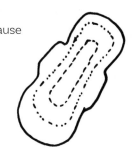

Panty liners

This is a smaller, thinner version of a sanitary towel – and, like a pad, they also come in a range of sizes and shapes. They are typically used at the beginning or end of a period when your flow is a lot lighter. They can also be worn outside of your usual period to offer reassurance in case you have any unexpected bleeding or excess discharge.

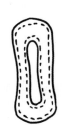

Menstrual cup

Like a tampon, a menstrual cup is inserted into your vagina. However, unlike a tampon or pad, it simply collects the menstrual blood – it doesn't absorb it. You insert it into the vagina by folding it into a 'C' shape, then allow it to unfold into its natural cup shape inside you. To remove, you just pinch the base and slide it on out.

A menstrual cup differs from a lot of other period products because it's reusable. It can be emptied, washed and reused every four to eight hours, and can be used while swimming or exercising. It's environmentally friendly too! If you are considering ways to help reduce the waste you produce, then using a menstrual cup is a good way to start – it lasts for a few years before you need to replace it, and can hold up to three times more blood than pads or tampons.

Period pants

Another sustainable and **reusable** alternative to pads or tampons is a pair of period pants. Essentially, they are underwear made from special material that absorbs your blood, and you can wash and wear them again and again. If you are worried about leaking, you can even wear period pants in addition to your tampon or pad for extra protection.

10 things you didn't know about periods

Kasey Robinson (she/her), period activist and founder of Proud of My Period

1. Periods are normal and healthy.

That might seem obvious, but there is still a lot of shame and stigma surrounding periods. Remember, they are not something that needs to be hidden or to feel embarrassed about. Your period is your monthly reminder that your body is working and doing its job.

2. Everyone's period is unique.

Whether you bleed a lot or a little, if you prefer tampons over pads, or if you need tea and a hot water bottle to alleviate your period pains – all of that is OK. Everyone is different. Talk about your periods, and not just with your mum but with anyone who will listen. Learning that there is no one way to have your period is part of normalising them for yourself and everyone else in society.

3. Not everyone can afford their periods.

Period poverty is a global and local issue. Many women and people who menstruate still don't have the means to buy the products they need each month. In the UK if you're using non-reusable period products, the average lifetime cost of having a period is £4,800 (Bloody Good Period). Not a joke.

4. We don't ever get a proper period education.

Did anyone ever sit you down at school and tell you what's inside a pad or tampon? Or have you ever had anyone explain how to identify when something isn't right with your period, and that experiencing severe pain isn't normal? Even if you know the answers to these, you're only scraping the surface. There is so much more we should learn about periods, but the education just isn't up to speed. We deserve to know how to take care of our bodies.

5. Period products are a necessity, not a luxury.

Think about it: you're at work, the cinema or in a restaurant. There's toilet paper, soap sometimes even hand cream, basically all of the things a person without a period needs. So, what about the rest of us? Well, nada. Period products aren't free in the places that they should be.

6. You should never flush your pad or tampon. Always bin it. Always.
Tons of period product waste goes into British toilets every year, and water companies waste so much money unclogging irrigation systems. Binning your (plastic free) period products can have a positive impact on the environment.

7. Tracking your period doesn't just mean tracking the days you bleed.
It's important to track every day in your cycle. That means your moods, the consistency of your discharge and then - when your period arrives - your blood loss. Your body is sending you important messages and knowing how to read them will help you manage your health better.

8. If you had all your periods in a row you would bleed for 6 years.
5 days a month x 12 months x 40 years. Over 6 whole years of having a period. It's not a vibe.

9. Black women and people who menstruate are poorly represented in the period activism space.
When it comes to period activism, Black women are rarely the ones seen in the media as leading the conversation. But, there are many Black women doing their part for better representation in this space. So remember, Black women don't just receive aid, we give it out too.

10. Periods aren't dirty, but the language we use around them makes it seem that way.
'Feminine hygiene products'?, 'Sanitary items'? I know you've heard phrases like these before. Not to mention all the code words for you period; *'on the rag'*, *'time of the month'*. Guess what? Tampons are tampons and pads are pads so that's what we're calling them. Oh, and your period doesn't need a code word. It hasn't committed a crime!

On endometriosis

Fiona Timba (she/her), solicitor and founder
of podcast Parts, Clarts and Hearts

I still remember when I started my period. I was twelve years old and getting ready for PE. In the days leading up to this moment, I'd been having aches in my tummy. My mum suspected it was my period, and so she made me a little period pack – a cute pencil-case-sized bag that contained sanitary towels. She taught me how to stick the pad in my underwear, talked me through what to expect and told me not panic. In spite of her prep, I still cried – not because it hurt, but because there was blood coming out of my bloody vagina (no pun intended)!

For the first few years, I had 'normal' periods, but when I was about fifteen or sixteen, things started to change. The cramps became more prominent, sometimes I'd be really faint. I'd often take days off from school due to the pain. You know when you watch a film or TV show of someone giving birth and they teach them how to breathe then squeeze? That's what my period became like – I'd be curled on my bed trying to breathe through the pain.

As the years progressed, so did the pain – and the amount of blood! I often had to sit on the toilet and free bleed, letting the clots and blood just come out. I'll never forget the time I went to an event hosted by the Lord Mayor of London and, just as the Lord Mayor began his speech, my whole body went numb and I felt the blood going through my tampon, through the pad and start trickling down my leg.

I spent the next thirteen years being told by doctors that I just had bad period pains or dysmenorrhea. I had scans, ultrasounds, transvaginal scans, MRIs, but everything was clear, so I was told nothing was wrong. I started to question if I had a low pain threshold, or even if it was all in my head. None of the medication prescribed helped, and being on the pill made everything worse.

When I was around twenty-seven, I realised I had endometriosis. I vividly remember sitting on the tube, reading an article about Lena Dunham's experience with endometriosis. She described exactly what I was experiencing: being unable to walk, work or sit, crouching on the floor in agony, suffering sleepless nights, sitting over the toilet, leaking, having to change my tampon every two hours. By the time I got off the tube, I was crying. My enemy had a name!

Endometriosis is a condition where tissue that is similar to the lining of the uterus is found *outside* the uterus. Each month, the tissue sheds just like your womb lining, but there is nowhere for the blood to go, so the area becomes inflamed.

It was another two years before I was medically diagnosed. My GP kept telling me it couldn't be endometriosis because my scans were clear. But I had read online that scans can't diagnose endometriosis – only a laparoscopic surgery can. I decided I wanted to see a specialist.

Luckily, I found someone. I remember shaking at my first appointment. But the doctor was kind and asked me questions, such as what type of pain I had, and what my bowel movements were like. Within a week, I'd been sent for an investigatory laparoscopy and been diagnosed with stage four endometriosis.

I'd like to say that was the end of it, but unfortunately endometriosis is a chronic condition which flares up. You can learn to manage the pain, but the key is really getting a diagnosis early so that you can prevent it from getting worse.

If you find yourself with more than three of these symptoms, speak to your doctor. You can also find support from charities such as Endometriosis UK. Last but not least, there are many wonderful women online sharing their experiences and who would be more than willing to provide an ear to listen – just search the #endometriosis tag.

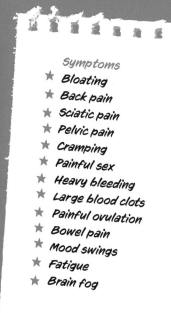

Symptoms
* Bloating
* Back pain
* Sciatic pain
* Pelvic pain
* Cramping
* Painful sex
* Heavy bleeding
* Large blood clots
* Painful ovulation
* Bowel pain
* Mood swings
* Fatigue
* Brain fog

Sex talk

Masturbation

Due to cultural and religious beliefs, or your families' personal views, the subject of female masturbation can often be considered taboo or even forbidden. And as big sis, I'm not here to pass judgement on your family's values. However, I believe it is important that we go there. So here goes … **Masturbation is the act of touching your body or your genitals for sexual pleasure.**

Often, girls are left out of the masturbation conversation. **Let's keep it real.** Whenever sex or anything pleasurable is discussed, it's usually for the benefit of the opposite sex. While the fact that boys might have wet dreams or 'morning wood' is widely talked about, not enough is said about the fact that we girls have sexual urges and desires too. Often, we are made to feel as though we need to remain 'pure' and 'virginal', and that anything sex-related is dirty.

Well, I'm telling you now, masturbating is perfectly normal and you shouldn't be embarrassed or ashamed for having sexual thoughts. Touching your body doesn't make you a terrible person. Done in private, whenever you feel like it, it's actually one of the safest ways to engage your desires and a natural way of discovering and exploring your body.

So you're ready for a relationship?

Entering into relationships and engaging in sexual activity isn't just about how old or mature you think you are. You don't just turn sixteen and BOOM, you are automatically ready for a relationship or sex.

It's important to consider your relationship with the person you want to be intimate with. Can you trust each other, communicate well and make each other feel safe? And, as embarrassing as having a boyfriend or girlfriend may seem, **healthy relationships aren't secret ones.** Being able to tell your parents or guardians that you are in a relationship is all part of the process of growing up. And, as adults, they may be able to pick up or issues that you may not yourself have much experience with yourself particularly when it comes to **red flags.** More on this shortly.

Some of you may be reading this and feel uncomfortable as you know your parents won't support your choice to have a partner. Even if they are harmless. I understand that too. In situations where your parents aren't that supportive, I recommend reaching out to another adult you trust. Despite how close me and my mum are, I wish I had been confident enough to tell her things I was experiencing in my relationships. It would have saved a lot of confusion, heartbreak and wasted time. It's only now that I actually understand why my mum kept telling me to 'face my books'.

At the end of the day, you're going to do what you want with who you want, no matter what I say. I've been there. I've got the T-shirt. In all the colours. Despite that fact, **one thing I wish I had known** was how to identify patterns of abuse or indicators that someone didn't have my best interests at heart.

At times, behaviour that I thought meant a person really liked me – I mean *really* liked me – was actually a warning of what was to come. It's so easy to end up in a situation where your boo gets jealous because you're spending time with other people, and they just want you all to themselves. Or they don't want you going to certain places or wearing certain things because they worry about how other people will behave or treat you. Perhaps they get really angry with you, but say it's because they love you so much. Or maybe you feel like you have to be careful of how you speak to them to ensure it doesn't cause a negative reaction. These are all **red flags** – signals that someone's behaviour could be toxic and abusive.

Here are some other red flags to look out for:

★ They don't let you speak.

✳ They don't listen to what you have to say.

★ They constantly judge you and others.

★ They only talk about themselves.

✳ They try and pressure or guilt trip you into doing things you don't want to do.

★ They make you feel like you owe them or you need to 'repay' them because they have been kind to you or given you gifts.

★ They force you into saying 'yes' because they react negatively when you say 'no'. This does not need to be anger or shouting; they could become extremely sad or resentful, resulting in them ghosting you or refusing to communicate.

✳ They make you justify why you don't want to do something.

Mother and daughter on domestic violence, coercive control and red flags

Melanie Brown (she/her), one fifth of the Spice Girls – one of the best selling girl groups of all-time

I wasn't very interested in school. I would daydream through a lot of lessons because learning about algebra, fractions and the biological make-up of a plant didn't really interest me. It didn't seem to have much meaning or relevance to my life. But the older I have got, the more experience of life I have had, I am now passionate about being part of the education system and teaching children something very important that I have learnt.

For ten years, I was in a very unhappy marriage. I was with a man who told me I was fat and ugly, and generally made me feel terrible about myself. He would take my phone and check it. He took control of all my finances, even though when we met I had a lot of money and he had next to nothing. I knew I was unhappy, but I didn't know that what I was living through was something called 'coercive control' – which is when someone completely takes control of their partner, telling them what they should do, wear, pay for, how to be with their children and how they should change their body.

I'm a really strong woman. I was successful. I had lots of friends. But I let this man into my life and a few years on I was really unhappy, I had very few friends and I had lost touch with my family. All I did was work, and I started to become very self-destructive because I thought I was a fake, a failure and a mess.

I want there to be lessons in schools where girls are taught that if you meet a guy who seems lovely and charming, but he starts asking to look at your phone or telling you what to wear or putting you down – walk away. If a man makes you feel bad, tells you things you have done that he says are wrong and then blames you for not understanding, this is called 'gas-lighting' and it's how someone can actually make you feel like you are going mad. Were you really flirting with another boy? Were you really laughing about him with your friends? You start to question everything because someone else is making you feel like everything you do is wrong.

I would like boys to be educated too – made to understand how this makes a woman feel and the effect it has on her and her family. It causes so much pain and suffering and can lead to terrible things happening behind closed doors. When I wrote my memoir, I was shown a piece of paper that I thought was just a timeline of my relationship with this man. I was wrong. It was a list of things to look for in an abusive relationship and it had been printed by a domestic violence organisation. I wish I had seen that piece of paper in school. I would like it to be put up on every toilet door in schools, restaurants, nightclubs, cinemas. That, to me, is real education.

Phoenix Brown, entrepreneur

The main thing I would want for a kid who has witnessed any form of domestic violence or abusive behaviour in the home, is to know that it is not their fault. It's really hard being a child when you know something isn't right, when you see things in your house that you know are wrong. It's easy to tell a child that they should talk to someone about what is happening, but I was that child and often this can be really complicated because the situation is so delicate. Children feel so helpless, and it's that helplessness that makes them feel it somehow is their fault. It's not. It never is. I wish I had known about organisations like Women's Aid, where they know exactly what to do and exactly what women – and men in some cases – are going through. I wish I had known there were places that would look after mums and children, and that it would be okay to discuss everything – because you have to be able to talk about things with your friends, or maybe in the future with a therapist. And I wish I had known that eventually things would change and get better, and that I'd be in a place where I could finally see my family start to heal.

We can stop if you want: Consent

At some point in your teenage years or early adulthood, you may start to form romantic relationships where there are physical acts that require your consent. These can range from holding hands, kissing, touching, exchanging sexual pictures or texts, right up to sexual intercourse.

On a basic level, **consent involves one person voluntarily giving permission for an act to happen.** Consent requires honest, open discussion and understanding about what both people are comfortable with. Consent isn't about one person making demands and the other resisting or accepting. It's continued, respectful, safe communication. Rather than consent being focused on what you don't want to do, see it as a conversation about what you and your partner *do* want to do. Consent is clear, enthusiastic and freely given. Consent should be clear not just through verbal cues, but non-verbal cues such as body language too. Consent isn't repeatedly asking someone to do something until they say yes. 'No' doesn't mean 'not now' or 'maybe later'. Getting someone to agree because they are under duress or scared doesn't mean you have consent either. Coercion isn't consent. If you have to push someone into doing something, that isn't consent. Consent doesn't require pressure. Consent cannot be obtained by bullying or through force. Consent can't be obtained by blackmail, intimidation or harassment. Or by begging or making comparison to what 'everyone' else is apparently doing.

> **Consent isn't just something only occurs in romantic relationships. It's something we should be practising in every interaction.**

Remember, communication is key – don't assume everything is OK just because the other person hasn't said no.

Flirting doesn't equal consent. Spending time with someone alone isn't consent. Being in a relationship with someone doesn't mean you automatically have consent. Receiving a picture from someone also doesn't mean they automatically consent to it being shared.

If someone is unenthusiastic, seems unsure or is unresponsive then they aren't giving their consent. If someone is sleeping, unconscious, drunk or high, they can't give consent.

Silence isn't consent. If someone is resisting, you don't have their consent.

And just so we are clear, **consent can be withdrawn at any time.** As your activities change, consent should be given every time – consent is an ongoing, forever-evolving conversation and a required point of communication.

Someone may be OK with you holding their hand or kissing them, but that doesn't mean you can touch them anywhere else. Consent isn't only needed for sexual intercourse – it's needed for anything sexual or physical. If the person can't say yes, or hasn't had an opportunity to say yes, then it's a no. Consent requires both parties to agree and have a clear understanding of what they are agreeing to.

Make sure you get consent EVERY time. Just because your partner has agreed to do something 100 times before, it is still your responsibility to ask the 101st time. Remember, everyone has autonomy over their own body, and you are not obligated or guaranteed to access to it. Period.

It is important that we normalise asking whether someone is comfortable with us engaging in contact with them. This ensures that you continually respect each other's boundaries.

Sex education

Safe, consensual sex isn't dirty, unclean or embarrassing. The majority of us are here because of it!

Now, I'm not going to have the big birds and the bees talk with you. Frankly, you and I both know that you probably know more about sex than I do! I'm sure you have watched enough episodes of *Love Island* and rapped along to enough Megan Thee Stallion songs to have a vague understanding of what goes where and how. I really just want to ensure that you're informed, you remain safe and you make good decisions.

DISCLAIMER

* The age of consent to any form of sexual activity is sixteen.

* It's illegal to share or ask for nudes or sexual pictures from anyone under the age of eighteen.

* Free contraception and advice is available from your GP or local sexual health clinic.

* Remember, these rules are in place to protect young people, not to criminalise or demonise them for the choices they make.

Sex is a weird one. I vaguely remember asking my mum where babies came from and she very calmly explained to me what sex was. But I don't distinctly remember how I found out about anything else. I don't recall ever being told about the pill or how to make safe sexual health choices.

When I was in school, sex education was really **scientific and boring.** Our biology teacher taught us about reproduction and then she demonstrated putting a condom on a weird plastic penis thing. That was it. There were no discussions about love. Same-sex relationships. Consent. What it felt like. Or even different types of contraception. It was literally: this is a vagina; this is a penis; aged sixteen, you can legally have sex; this is how you put a condom on. The end.

Useless. Unhelpful. Unbothered

We spent the majority of the lesson gossiping about who was already doing it, catching up on forgotten homework and thinking of the most ridiculous names to give our future babies. But sex talk really shouldn't be so dry and uninteresting. It makes sex seem clinical and awkward, and can lead to you feeling uncomfortable about discussing sex or exploring your body. Or it can have the opposite effect and make you curious about what really goes on when the penis isn't made from plastic!

Personally, I reckon adults often worry about discussing sex with young people because even at their big big age they are still embarrassed to discuss it with one another! The majority of adults probably think you'll just figure it out yourself – like they did. A lot of parents worry that talking about sex brings you one step closer to doing it. Others may feel it's something you should wait until you're older to discuss for religious or cultural reasons. And, a lot of the time, parents don't want us to make the mistakes they did. They might never admit it, but they know how we feel and why we do the things that we do. But their responsibility as main caregivers is to ultimately keep you safe and out of harm's way. One day you are a babygirl playing with a toy truck or Barbie doll, and the next you're a big big woman going on your first date.

> Did you make your Barbie and Ken dolls lay down together naked – or was that just me lol? When I think about it, a lot of us have probably known about and been curious about sex for longer than we started asking questions about it.

It might be difficult to talk to your parents about sex. Maybe they have already accused you of having sex and made you feel bad about it. Or maybe they've assumed you have a boyfriend when you actually have a girlfriend. Or they've avoided your questions on how to stay safe if and when you do decide to take things further. However, despite what it may seem, your parent's reaction may be more about them feeling uncomfortable than actually being unwilling to talk to you about sex. Sometimes parents make these mistakes because they're ignorant, and sometimes they say the wrong thing out of pure panic. You don't get given a manual when you get older telling you how to deal with these situations.

> I guess that's why we wrote Grown. If you feel as though you aren't getting the help you require, you can reach out to several organisations that have been set up to assist young Black people, including LGBTQIA+ groups, and safe spaces for those of you who may not feel comfortable discussing your sexuality with anyone you know.

Contraception

Contraception is used for two reasons – to prevent unwanted pregnancy and to protect against STIs. More on this later. They aren't always fail-safe, but if used properly they will do a better job than praying and wishing for the best.

According to the NHS, there are roughly fifteen types of contraception available in the UK. For professional advice on what will work best for your needs and your body, visit your GP or a sexual health clinic, but I'm going to give you a brief overview of some of the most popular types:

Male and female condoms: These contraceptives place a physical barrier between the egg and the sperm, preventing pregnancy and exposure to certain STIs. A male condom is placed over the penis, and a female condom is inserted into the vagina.

Diaphragm: This is similar to a female condom, but should be used with spermicide – a gel that kills sperm. When placed inside your vagina, it acts kind of like a cap covering your cervix (the passageway that connect your vagina to your womb) preventing any sperm from passing through. But it doesn't protect you from STIs.

The pill: There are many different versions of the pill, but most contain a combination of artificial female hormones known as oestrogen and progesterone. The pill prevents ovulation, aka the release of an egg during your monthly cycle. (Think back to the periods section of this chapter and this may all start clicking.) No egg release = no egg for sperm to fertilise = no babies. But the pill also doesn't protect you from STIs.

Contraceptive implant, injection or patch: The implant is a plastic rod that is placed under the skin of your upper arm and releases pregnancy-preventing hormones into your body. The injection releases the same hormones directly into your bloodstream, and the patch is like a plaster that releases the hormones into your skin. All three need to be re-upped after a particular amount of time, ranging from one week for the patch, thirteen weeks for the injection to three years for the implant. None of them stops the spread of STIs.

Morning after pill: This pill is an emergency form of contraception, that can prevent pregnancy after you have had unprotected sex, or if one of the methods above has failed. There are two types – depending on which pill you get, have either up to three days or five days to take it. The sooner you take it, the more effective it is. The morning after pill does not work if you are already pregnant. And if you continue to have unprotected sex after taking it, you can still get pregnant. No surprises here: it doesn't protect you from STIs.

Most contraceptives have a high level of protection if used properly, but – I'll be honest with you – the only way to 100 per cent guarantee you won't get pregnant or get an STI is to not have sex at all. So, if you care about your sexual health and you want to have sex, I recommend you double up by using a condom in conjunction with another form of contraception that works for you.

If you are seriously considering having sex and believe you are emotionally mature enough to do so, then it's important that you are able to have open and honest conversations with the person you wish to have sex with – as well as with a parent, guardian or sexual health professional. Yes, I bet you didn't think I was going to say that. But trust me, while it is proper embarrassing, if you're grown enough to do it, you're grown enough to discuss it too. Being open and honest means that you can get the right support, and ensures that you aren't Googling 'Am I pregnant?' just because you kissed a boy.

Not today: the excuses
you should never accept

Having sex with someone is a big deal, and there are certain things you may not recognise that could be major red flags. As big sis, I wouldn't be me if I didn't tell you in advance the lies that people will use to get away with not using protection. Don't fall for it babygirl!

'You're so sexy / peng / beautiful, let's just do it.' Yes, you are beautiful. Gorgeous in fact. But no one is so nice that they can get away with not using protection. STIs don't discriminate.

'It feels so much better without it.' Maybe it does. But it also feels better having a lie-in and not having to do a morning feed before school.

'I'm clean.' RED FLAG. Even if they don't have an STI, how can they be confident you don't? This is a major red flag and indicates they don't care about their sexual health or yours.

'Why don't you trust me?' Trust has nothing to do with it miss mamas. They can't just pick and choose who to transmit STIs to.

'I just don't want to use protection.' Great! They are honest and trustworthy. They are also selfish and don't care about your feelings or your needs. Tell that boy or girl 'bye'.

'I don't have any.' Stop the lying please. Contraceptives are free to under-twenty-fives and easy to obtain. As someone engaging in sexual activity, it is your responsibility that you stay strapped up. Also, Tesco is open twenty-four hours.

'They don't fit me.' Fake news! Sorry, but a stretched condom is around 18 inches and can fit over someone's head.

'I'll pull out.' Despite being free and seeming like a really smart idea at the time, withdrawal isn't a safe or effective contraceptive method. You can't just stop sperm travelling to an egg by pulling out when you feel like it. It also doesn't protect you from STIs. Also, everyone I went to school with who did this got pregnant. Pull-out method's success rate? 0/10.

'You won't get pregnant if I ...' You *can* get pregnant if you don't use protection. There isn't a position or a prayer that can save you. Don't trust him, sis!

Finally, you cannot use a plastic bag or a piece of clingfilm in place of a condom. I know you were thinking it!

STIs

Sexually Transmitted Infections (STIs) can be passed from one person to another through sexual contact. That includes vaginal, anal and oral sex.

STIs **aren't always curable.** They can cause things like infertility. Often there are no symptoms, but if there are, they can display themselves as sores, rashes, lumps, itching, tingling, smelly discharge or pain when you wee. You may notice what looks like black powder or pearl-shaped balls in your pants – that's pubic lice, aka crabs. Similar to nits.

Infections such as these don't just disappear without medical attention. So please **don't ignore the signs.** At the end of the day, anyone can get an STI, and the only way of knowing if you do is by ensuring you have regular check-ups prior to engaging in sex, and being open about your sexual activity with your partners.

Smear Test

This quick and painless test is the best way of catching any abnormal cells in the cervix before they can develop into cancer. A smear test is for anyone who has a vagina. This includes transgender men. It is important to check the health and status of your cervix if you have one, regardless of your gender identity.

The main infection that a smear test is looking for is Human Papillomavirus or HPV is a viral infection that can cause genital warts or cervical cancer. There are more than 100 varieties of HPV and some are classed as low-risk or high-risk, but most infections do not lead to cancer. However, nearly 99.7% of cervical cancer cases are caused by HPV.

HPV is very common and can be caught very easily through any type of skin-to-skin or sexual contact, including touching. Most people will have an HPV infection at some point, however as there generally are no symptoms, your body will usually get rid of it naturally without any treatment.

In the UK, girls and boys aged twelve to thirteen are routinely offered vaccinations to protect against four types of high-risk HPVs. Remember, the HPV vaccination doesn't stop you getting pregnant and it won't protect you from other STIs.

PREGNANCY:
Your body, your choice

Teen pregnancy is often spoken about negatively. But *Grown* is a judgement-free zone – Natalie and I are just here to empower you to make good choices.

You may have had unprotected sex. You may have done everything that you can to stay safe. Yet you have still become pregnant. **Don't panic.** You haven't made a mistake. It's just another path on your life journey. You might be scared. Anxious. Excited. Happy. Sad. You might not know how you feel right now. But you do have some options:

★ Continue with your pregnancy and keep your baby

✱ Continue with your pregnancy and give the baby up for adoption

★ Have an abortion, also known as a termination

There are lots of charities and services to help support young mums. But whatever you decide, remember, **there is no right or wrong decision** here. It's your body and your choice. Do not feel pressurised to make a decision that doesn't serve you. It's also important to point out that having a child isn't a death sentence. In fact, many of us have parents who were teenagers when we were born. It's nothing to feel ashamed of and your age won't prevent you from being a good parent. Equally, there is nothing to be ashamed of if you do have a termination. You have to do what is right for you at the time and make your own, informed choices.

Becoming a mum

Sorayah July (she/her), educator

Like most teens, I really felt I was invincible aged seventeen. I was smart and focused at sixth form, whilst still maintaining my party girl, Bad B lifestyle. I was ready to start uni the following year where I could amplify my current lifestyle x10. I had plans to go to university as far away as possible and invite my hometown boyfriend over at weekends, just like in the American movies.

My boyfriend and I had been together a while, and yes, we were having sex. I hadn't asked anyone for advice about it beforehand. I'd had PSHE lessons so I knew what contraception was, but I just felt too embarrassed to go anywhere and ask for it. My boyfriend usually had condoms with him anyway so I didn't think I really needed to be prepared. Until he didn't. But he was going to pull out, and that method is known for its success rate, right? Wrong. Melissa has already mentioned that everyone she knew who used this method ended up pregnant, and I am one of them.

While life didn't turn out a million miles from my initial plans, many things did change. Yes, I still went to uni. Yes, I was still a Bad B (it's a mindset, not an image.) Yes, I still had the hometown boyfriend. But now there was an additional person in the mix – and there was also no point in calling him a 'hometown' boyfriend anymore because neither of us ended up leaving said hometown. In fact, we just all crammed into my childhood bedroom – boyfriend, baby and me.

When I first found out I was pregnant, I was worried but, surprisingly, didn't have a meltdown. I think a large part of me was excited. I hadn't had it easy over the previous few years of my life, and I was looking forward to feeling needed by a tiny human. That's a part of teenage pregnancy that you don't often hear about. You hear about the tears, the panic, the disaster stories, but not much about the positive things that come out of it. You usually don't hear about what was happening in that teenager's life before the pregnancy arrived. You also don't hear much about how your life is impacted once the baby arrives, or once that baby turns into a toddler, or a child, or a teenager – and how, before you know it, you're giving them a copy of *Grown* to prepare them for what is to come.

That's the thing. It's not just about changing dirty nappies or staying up all night trying to get the bottle to the right temperature. It's not even just about missing nights out with friends, because, while your time with friends is limited, if you have a good support network you can have some time off and be a 'normal' teen here and there. But your whole lifestyle changes. Every decision you make has to involve your child. No, you can't get those extra-long acrylic nails because you might get a bit of baby poo caught in them during a nappy change (yes, this really happens.) No, you can't get those ultra-long lash extensions because your baby will grab at them. No, you can't go to uni and stay in halls with friends because you're not just one student, you're a whole family. No, you can't spend your last pennies on that festival or girls' trip because your child needs new school shoes. This list is endless.

That's not to say that I regret being a mum. Not at all. But I know that if I had made more careful choices earlier on, I could have been a more rounded person with actual life experiences before becoming a mum. And I could have had so much more to offer to my child.

Trust your body

There is more to say about bodies, puberty, relationships and sex than I've covered in the pages here. But, hopefully what you've read has given you some honest and useful advice to help you navigate the physical changes that occur when you transition from girl to woman. Don't be afraid to ask questions and talk to people you trust about what's happening and how you're feeling. As girls and women, we've all been there. All the hair, lumps, bumps and bits are perfectly normal – and beautiful too.

Yours faithfully

Your beliefs, morals and thinking big

By Natalie

Our religion and cultural beliefs find a seat at every one of the tables in our life. These things shape our family, our traditions and our community's expectations of us. Our religion and our beliefs can affect everything, from what we wear and who we are allowed to spend time with, to what we study at school and what career path we take. Religion can also be used to justify cultural beliefs and practices that have nothing to do with religion at all. This isn't always easy to accept, especially when the religion you've been part of since childhood is unlikely to be something you've chosen for yourself.

'Whatever faith or religion makes you a better, peaceful, more loving, compassionate person is the one you should choose & practise.'
Janelle Monáe [1]

I grew up in a strong, loving Christian family. My grandad was a pastor at a Jamaican Pentecostal church, and a lot of my family are still really involved in the churches they attend now. As a young girl, my church congregation was my community and they certainly helped shape my morals and my identity as a Black British woman. Growing up in church definitely made me who I am today, but I have conflicting feelings about religion, faith and church.

Being part of a religious group or community can make you a target of discrimination, especially if it means you dress a certain way or cover your head outside of your home. People who don't practise religion can be very vocal about criticising the religious practices of others. They may dismiss religion as something insignificant, or buy into the negative stereotypes that surround different religions. Suffering discrimination due to something so integral to your identity is painful. I remember how fearful I was about being mocked because my family was religious, or because I couldn't eat certain things or do some of the things my friends could. I tried so hard to downplay how much I went to church, or what my family believed because I didn't want to feel different or seem restricted in ways my friends weren't. I attached so much shame to my religion. Feeling excluded like this can be really upsetting. Trying to figure out who you are and what is important to you is difficult enough without being excluded for something that forms part of your identity.

Religion played a main role in every scene of my life, and while sometimes I loved this, at other times I felt very frustrated. I couldn't do what everyone else was doing and my FOMO was real. Even if I wasn't really interested in doing some of the things I was missing out on, the fact that it wasn't my choice jarred me. I felt that religion was something I had to participate in, even though, if I was honest with myself, I didn't really understand or care for it. Some of the teachings and practices did not seem logical to me, and rarely were they backed up by evidence.

Growning up, many of the messages that I received about my womanhood reinforced the stereotype that a woman's role in the church and at home was one of subordination to men. There seemed to be a real focus on policing how women dressed and behaved and, as usual, I don't remember the boys around me having such strict rules controlling what they did. Boys didn't seem to be victim to the harsh judgement of church elders over how they dressed or if they argued back, and they were never criticised for being too 'fast' or 'loose'.

When I saw or heard things at church like this that I didn't understand or agree with, **I wanted to ask why**, but I often held my tongue, assuming I wouldn't get the answers I needed. It felt like the word of a religious leader or, in my case, a church elder was rarely questioned or challenged because that person was a 'servant of God'. There were many times that I needed to express how I felt about what I was being taught at church, yet I didn't even feel like I could talk to my parents because they seemed to embrace these beliefs too.

Still, I wasn't sure that what I was being taught was the only way to live my life – but when you're told from childhood that behaving in a certain way has huge consequences, it can be **hard and scary** to go against that. However, I soon realised that a lot of what I was taught was morally correct was not necessarily about Christianity at all, it was more about the way in which my community practised it. To try and understand how I felt about my Christian upbringing, I had to teach myself how to separate cultural opinions and practices from religion, how to interpret the messages I was receiving and how to figure out what I believed in and stood for myself.

I know that my experiences are not unique. As Black women, we are more likely to grow up in a religious home. Even if your family doesn't go to a place of worship weekly, or consider themselves 'religious', there's a good chance that you are part of a community that has values and practices which are rooted in religion. So many of our moral values are influenced by our culture, and so you may feel the same pressures and restrictions on who you can be or what you can do even if you aren't religious. You may feel pressure to get married by a certain age, or feel you can't take the opportunities given to you because you are a girl who needs to grow into what those around you believe to be a 'good woman'. You may believe that as a girl from your culture you can't be who you truly want to be because you don't fit the description of a 'good girl'. You might feel you don't have the same freedoms as the boys your age in your family or your community. Whether or not we are religious, we all have to deal with being watched and judged by those around us. I get this. Growing up, I felt like the community that was raising me seemed to have very strong opinions on what I could and could not do, and even if I wasn't told this explicitly, I internalised those beliefs. And these beliefs didn't just fall away after time – they still impact me today.

In this chapter I am going to talk about the reality of growing up in a religious family and a tight-knit community, and consider how this can impact your identity and your value system. I'm going to give you some keys that will empower you to form your own beliefs and trust your own judgement. Your religion, your beliefs and your faith should be YOUR choice. But it takes courage to form your OWN beliefs, especially if those beliefs are different from those you were raised with.

Forming your own views may seem intimidating, but this is a part of becoming grown. Hopefully this chapter can help you understand how to make a decision about your spirituality or faith **when you feel the time is right.** However, you may never actually feel that you need to make such a decision. You might be happy to continue practising the religion you have grown up with, or you might not have questions about the beliefs of those around you. You may be happy not to be a part of any organised religion at all. **Wherever you're at, it's OK.**

BIG FACT

What I believe is what I believe, and what you believe is what you believe and we owe respect to everyone we interact with – even if we don't agree with each other's beliefs. We should not try to disprove someone else's faith or condemn or correct it. While all religions believe that they represent the true and correct way to live, there is no gold standard of faith or religion. We are all entitled to our own beliefs as long as our daily practices do not harm or hurt others.

Our history with religion

As Black people, our history with some of the major world religions is very complicated. Many of the religions Black people around the world now participate in were introduced to our ancestors through colonialism and slavery. And so, while religion provides comfort for us during difficult times, it is important to recognise that **it has also been used to control and silence us.**

Before colonialism, our ancestors had different religions and cultural practices. Nowadays, we aren't really taught about these religions and they are often dismissed as 'primitive', 'witchcraft' or 'backwards'. This is because when white people from the West took control of our ancestors' countries, they told them that the way they organised their societies and made decisions was 'backwards'. As a result, we were encouraged to turn away from these principles in order to embrace a more Western way of thinking.

> *'I've always been a woman of faith.'*
> **Lauren London** [2]

There are many traditional African and Afro-Caribbean religions and belief systems – including Obeah, the Yoruba faith and Santería to name but a few – that should be **respected** in the same way we respect and recognise Christianity, Judaism or Islam. Many of our ancestors practiced Obeah, a traditional Caribbean religion that follows a system of spiritual and healing practices that originate from West Africa. Many Black women today are returning to these religions as part of their personal spiritual journey, and using these practices as a way to reconnect with their culture and their ancestors. Some Black women say that this makes them feel empowered and more included than other mainstream religions. Honouring traditional spiritual practices can be seen as a way of preserving our collective history and identity – but that doesn't invalidate the religions that our communities practise today. These religions are still a huge part of our identity, and bring comfort, security and purpose to many people's lives.

But, before we get into this chapter any deeper, I want to explain what religion really is and why people sometimes differentiate between religion and faith – and how culture fits into the mix.

So, what is religion?

Religion is a belief in a superhuman power or being. It is usually underpinned by a system of beliefs and basic principles about our relationship with that higher power, God or Gods, how we should live our lives – from what we eat and how we dress to when we work and when we rest – and what happens after we pass away. Each religion has its own spiritual practices and forms of worship. Some religions have a holy book that sets out their particular principles – the Bible (Christianity), the Quran (Islam), the Tanakh (Judaism) are a few of the religious books you may have heard of. Some other religions have multiple holy texts, or their principles are communicated orally.

Many religions have different denominations (smaller groups within them) that all have slightly different practices and beliefs – think of the Roman Catholic, Protestant and Orthodox churches in Christianity, for example. Within each denomination there may also be sects (smaller groups again). Islam has many different sects, including Sunni, Kharijites and Shia.

'I hold that any religion that satisfies the individual urge is valid for that person.'
Zora Neale Hurston [3]

What is a faith?

A faith is a strong belief based on a spiritual conviction. It is much more personal than religion because it relies on how individuals feel and their personal connection with the world around them. For example, someone who identifies as religious may not have a personal relationship with the supernatural being connected to their religion, but they may still believe in its main messages. Equally, someone who doesn't participate in an organised religion may have a strong sense of spirituality and believe that there is a higher power with whom they want to build a strong relationship. Practices such as yoga, meditation, tarot reading and grounding are based on faith. Many people see prayer or journaling as a daily spiritual practice, and use them as a way to connect to a higher being, or as a way to seek guidance on what steps to take in their lives. However, often these people would not consider themselves religious in the traditional sense.

Where does culture come in?

Our culture is who we are as a group. It's our history, what we eat, how we dress, how we dance, how we love others, the way we speak. It is our essence and we should treasure and preserve it. The culture of our community plays a big part in helping us **form our beliefs.** And so, it is sometimes hard to tell where religion ends and culture starts, and there is usually a big overlap between the two.

When we have bad experiences with religion, this can often be down to the cultural practices, beliefs and actions of those in our religious community, rather than the principles of the religion itself. Some people uphold cultural behaviours and attitudes on the basis of religion, even if those things have nothing to do with religious principles at all.

Growing up, many of the church practices I followed, from what women were required to wear to what I believed others should or should not do – and even how we prayed – were not always strictly based on principles in the Bible. In fact, those things were actually more a part of Jamaican Pentecostal culture. As I grew, I learnt to understand the difference between religious principles and cultural beliefs.

Women and religion

One of the things that I found really tough growing up was the way women were spoken about and treated in church. My church family was held together by the hard work, service and sacrifice of generations of women, yet their hard work was rarely acknowledged, and there was a clear glass ceiling that stopped so many women from achieving significant leadership positions in the church. Even though the majority of the people who attended my church were Black women, it was nearly always a man preaching or teaching on Sunday morning. Meanwhile, I saw Black women cooking, cleaning, serving and looking after pastors. Don't get it twisted, there is nothing wrong with women serving others, as long as women are given the equal opportunity to lead, and men are also expected to serve.

There also seemed to be a real focus on policing **how women dressed** and behaved. We were told that our time as single women must be spent retaining our 'purity' as we waited for our husbands. Therefore, we shouldn't be seen in certain places with certain people, especially with boys from outside our families or other people outside of our community, because that is not what 'good' women from our religion, family, tribe, country or island do. Not only do these unhealthy restrictions make us feel self-conscious and limited, they teach our brothers, cousins and other men around us that we are **subordinate,** and that this is how they should continue to treat us.

What was so frustrating was that it wasn't just the men at church projecting these ideas – it was the women too! In fact, some of the comments the aunties and 'church mothers' made when I was a young girl still impact how I think about myself and my life to this day.

Unpicking your beliefs

As much as religion tends to promote humility and kindness, it can also be used to control others' behaviour and lifestyle, or to judge them for mistakes they've made. Far too often, I have seen people unfairly shamed and excluded because they supposedly fell short of the standards imposed by their religion.

Sometimes we accept beliefs we've been taught without really thinking them through. I am a strong believer in taking time to **figure out what you believe,** where this belief has come from and what the consequences of upholding that belief are. When thinking about your own principles, you can ask yourself the below questions and work through the answers to **make sure you understand** how your belief system is developing.

What is the belief?
This could be any moral or religious belief about how we should behave, hold ourselves or interact with others that you want to explore.

....

....

Where have I learnt this belief?
Where do you think this belief came from?
Were you taught this by someone else, for example?

....

....

How do I feel about this belief?
Do you feel comfortable with this belief?
Do you actually agree with it when you think about it deeply?

....

....

What is the impact of this belief on my life?
Does this belief affect how you feel or treat others?
Does it make you happy?

....

....

The above exercise is just a start. If you aren't entirely sure about certain beliefs you hold, take time and come back to this activity whenever you feel ready.

Question it

Don't feel that in order to truly follow a religion you always need to accept the status quo, and don't let anything stop you from standing by what you believe. If something you hear, see or read in church doesn't sit right with your spirit, **speak up** and **ask questions.** Questioning requires someone to give you a response and a justification for what they have said, done or asked you to do. You should be able to ask **as many questions as you need to,** and don't just accept it when someone answers you with, 'That's just the way it is.'

I know we are taught to respect our elders and part of that is often *not* questioning or giving backchat, but we owe it to ourselves to speak up and not to go along with what someone says if we are unsure. If someone doesn't want to answer your questions or explain, take that as a sign that you should not be doing anything with that person, please.

Questioning religious beliefs and practices doesn't mean that you don't respect or have faith in your religion, it just means that you're taking the time to understand it for yourself, so that you can make your own decisions. In fact, it will deepen your understanding. Knowledge and understanding are major keys - you might frustrate those around you (including your parents or guardians) but I would rather you question everything than trust someone you shouldn't, and suffer harm. Don't assume just because someone is a leader that everything they do is righteous or correct.

Trust is earned

People put a lot of trust in religious leaders who they believe have heard directly from God, and who are more 'spiritually advanced'. But religious leaders are human – they make mistakes, and can lie or manipulate just like anybody else.

A lot of people have experienced trauma within their religious communities. Many young Black girls have been subjected to emotional, physical and sexual abuse and even financial exploitation at the hands of their religious leaders or elders.

Now, I am not saying that your religious leader is corrupt or untrustworthy. I am saying that **it is OK to question what you are told** if it doesn't seem right to you. People shouldn't be trusted simply because they hold a position of leadership in your religious community, especially if their actions don't match up with their messaging.

Sometimes, we blindly follow people we trust because we believe they have our best interests at heart. It can be easy to get swept up in the hype and not understand what is really happening. Below are a few situations that should raise alarm bells.

IT'S A PROBLEM IF SOMEONE:

★ asks you to do something that they don't want you to tell your parents or carers about

★ threatens you with punishment if you do not do as they say

★ tries to persuade you to do something you believe is wrong

★ asks you to lie or manipulate someone else

★ does something that makes you feel uncomfortable

If you experience any of these things, tell an adult you trust straight away, whether that's a family member, teacher or one of the organisations I have listed at the end of this chapter.

Knowing what is RIGHT for you

We are all blessed with **intuition** – that feeling within ourselves that pipes up every time we need to make a big decision or choose a path in our lives. We need to trust that feeling when it comes to what we believe. You have the free will to investigate different religions, spiritual practices and ways of living – and, if this is an area in your life you want to grow in, take the time to get to know the path you are choosing for yourself.

I used to feel like developing my own spirituality was a competition. I didn't want to fall behind those around me or be a 'bad Christian', but I just couldn't force it. I had to take the time to figure things out for myself, to understand the life I wanted to live and the person I wanted to be. I had to accept that my beliefs were not always going to strictly align with the opinions of others, but that they were right for me. I remember being told that it was wrong to do certain things because they contradicted my religion, yet today some of these practices bring me the **greatest peace.** What matters is that YOU are content with who YOU are. We all need to understand the basic principles by which we want to guide our own lives. You have your own mind and you can take time to figure out what is right for you.

'In all your getting, get understanding.'
Jacqueline Woodson [3]

What centres me

Tobi Olujinmi, founder of W Talk Network

I grew up in a Christian home, and my mum made sure my siblings and I went to Church every Sunday, by fire by force. Like most people, as I hit my teenage years, I began exploring what I loved about the world and what I didn't. It was aged sixteen that I made a personal decision to pursue Christianity for myself, and not because my parents wanted me to. Since then, it has really impacted eeverything and become and integral part of my life. I started preaching, pretty much from aged sixteen, which strangely enough brought many a 'mandem' my way. I suppose they saw it as a challenge to try and break the 'Christian girl'. I believe that God is interested in the intricate details of my life, whether that meant a boy I was seeing, or my career path or how I raise my children. It truly centres me. Living my life connected to the One who created me and loved me first – everything else extends from that place.

Your moral compass

A moral compass is what helps us decide what is right or wrong. It is our **internal guide,** shaping how we understand the perspectives of others, how we interpret situations and how we make decisions on a day-to-day basis. Our moral compass is definitely influenced by our religion, faith and the culture we grew up in, as well as our families and the people we spend time with. However, it's important to remember that it isn't only defined by these things – it's mostly about what YOU feel is right. Thinking about the below questions will help you **explore** your moral compass:

What do you think is the difference between right and wrong is?

How do you want to be treated? And how do you want to treat others?

Who can you go to for moral guidance when you're unsure?

Who influences your beliefs? E.g. your mother, pastor or friends.

What's important to you? E.g. Family, kindness, compassion, God, helping those in need, community.

What rules do I want to live my life by?

E.g. Always try to make others' smile, listen to other people's opinions, stand up for those who can't stand up for themselves.

As we become grown, many of our experiences – including the things we see our friends, our sisters or people we love go through – will shift our beliefs and standpoints on so many different issues. **Our moral compass is constantly evolving.** What you write above is just a starting point, so you can see where you're currently at.

Staying true to yourself

It takes courage to be open and honest about how you feel about your religion and your culture, especially if they dictate that the way you live, who you are or who you love is wrong or immoral. So many of us **suffer in silence** and pretend to be something that we are not. We may even try to pray these parts of ourselves away – or worse, our family members and communities may try to pray or stamp them out of us. These experiences are so painful and can cause us to struggle with accepting or embracing who we really are.

We live in a world where we all want to be accepted, loved and embraced, but we **cannot compromise** who we are. Place your mental wellbeing at the centre of any decision you make about your beliefs. That may mean having to develop your faith on your own, focusing on what you believe and what your morality is, rather than sticking strictly to the rules or perceptions of an organised religion you do not agree with. You can't simply follow fashion when it comes to faith – ultimately, it's about **what works for you.**

Nothing is lost

Kafayat Okanlawon (she/her), author and founder of Feminist Focus, an online platform where women of colour can share their experiences

ORGANISATIONS YOU CAN SPEAK TO IF YOU NEED SUPPORT

- ★ The Children's Society
- ★ NSPCC
- ★ Karma Nirvana
- ✳ YoungMinds
- ✳ Rape Crisis

When reflecting on my spiritual journey I now see the gift it is to be raised in an Islamic household. When I was younger it was inconvenient having to attend Madrassa (Islamic school) every weekend, pray five times a day or wear a hijab, now I see how those acts taught me the importance of community, grounding and how I view beauty.

Regardless of where I am on my spiritual journey, I realise nothing is lost. Despite not going to mosque every Friday and my prayer peak tending to be during Ramadan, the teachings of Islam – love, grounding, offering, discipline and mission – will always be the basis I live my life from.

8 Got skills

Education, work experience and chasing your dream career

By Natalie

There is no limit to what you can achieve, and there is no set path for Black women. Regardless of what you are focusing on, in order to reach your goals, you need to have the right skills, experience and qualifications to get there.

You may feel **under pressure** to go to college or university because you think you need a 'good education' so you can get a good job. There is some truth in that. But that isn't going to guarantee that you get the right career for YOU. In this chapter, I am going to focus on taking the time to really consider what career could be best for you, and how understanding your **natural strengths** and **passions are** vital in making that important decision – plus the steps you can take to get there.

'Trust yourself. Think for yourself. Act for yourself. Speak for yourself. Be yourself. Imitation is suicide.'
Marva Collins [1]

When I picked my GCSE options, I wanted to study food technology, but my dad crossed it off my list because it wasn't a 'serious' academic subject. I did statistics instead, which I hated. I wasn't even that upset at the time because I thought I understood where he was coming from. But to this day, cooking new recipes and trying new cuisines is one of my favourite hobbies, and I still cook for people every chance I get – so who knows where studying food technology could have led me? Your parents or guardians might be pressuring you to follow a certain route or study a subject that they believe will put you on a 'secure' career path. But if you know you are passionate about something, fight for it and don't give up easily.

It's not just our parents who can influence us to do something that is not true to what we want in our heart – our friends and peers can too. Don't feel pressured to do something just because you think it's what 'successful' people do. Sometimes, we are naturally talented at things we **take for granted,** and we fight to be good at or like the things that everyone else is doing because we think that's the way forward. Now, I'm not saying only do what comes easily to you, because anything you truly want is worth fighting for, but why kill yourself to like business studies just because lots of your friends do, when you know deep down you love history? Why force yourself to like maths when your passion is really for art? Make it make sense!

What matters is that you know what you are good at, what you like and what your strengths are. Always be honest about why you want to do something.

If a career interests you because you want to make money, that's OK. But it's important to think about all the other factors that will impact your day-to-day life too. Take it from me, it is hell on this Earth to kill yourself to get a 'dream' job role that is completely incompatible with who you are and the life you want to live. The best career is one where you are using the natural talents and abilities you have to do something you care about.

And just so you know, it is OK to be unsure about what career or industry you want to work in. You also don't have to stick to one career for your whole life. It's **never too late** to try new things or get a new job.

This chapter is designed to help you start thinking about what **options** are out there for you. Even if you know exactly what you want to study and what career you want to pursue, you can use these pages to take time to think about your choices and check that the path you have chosen plays to your strengths and truly works for you.

'When you're in your lane, there's no traffic.'
Ava DuVernay [2]

Finding a path that fits **YOU** perfectly

Your career is an integral part of your life, and, while it doesn't define you, not picking the right career can really bring you unhappiness. Working will take up a lot of your time and so it's important to think about what you want to spend your time actually doing – your chosen career will fit in with the life you are building for yourself.

Don't worry if a career doesn't spring instantly to mind. Just take a step back and breathe. Don't be anxious, just be open-minded. It is hard to know where to start, but we have a few ideas to help you get yourself into the right mindset.

Let's start by thinking about what subjects YOU are naturally good at both inside and outside of education, what YOU enjoy doing and talking about, and the things that YOU do in other areas of your life, such as at home or in your friendships. Just because something doesn't seem academic or directly related to a career doesn't mean that it isn't.

There is space below for you to **create a mind map** with the things you are good at, the things you care about and the things you like doing. Include anything you want! If you are a great cook and love cooking, write that down. If you love listening to and solving other people's problems, then that's something to go on the list as well. If, when it comes to making plans, you are the organised one who gets everyone where they need to be on time, that should also go on the list.

Do you like creating things from scratch, or do you prefer to work with an order or a system that is already in place? Are you the person who figures out how to use a new app or software with ease? Are you creative and bursting with new ideas?

> Focus on YOUR strengths and what YOU like doing. Nothing is irrelevant or too small, and we all have hidden talents or passions we can work with.

Your career mind map

Things you are good at

Things you like doing

Things you care about

Once you've finished, have a look at what you've written down. I bet there are things that you didn't even think about being relevant to your career before!

Now, don't expect a career path to instantly jump out at you based on what you have mapped out. This is just about **finding out what excites you.** Once you know what you enjoy doing and where your strengths lie, you can start looking at different industries and job roles that make use of your talents and passions.

There may be some things on your map that you are good at, but have no interest in. That's OK. Even though I did really well in sciences at school, I never enjoyed them and so I knew from the jump that a career that required me to study a traditional science subject was not the one. Be honest with yourself and trust your intuition. Remember to think about what you can see yourself doing every day and truly enjoying, and put this at the centre of your decision-making process. If there's something on your map you know isn't for you, feel free to strike it through.

Find your focus

Now you have your mind map in the bag, let's start thinking about how you pick a career. You don't have to be really specific about what you are going to do just yet. You might know that you want to work in beauty because that industry excites you, but that doesn't mean you have to pick exactly what you want to do and stick to it. The key to figuring what you want to do is to do your research.

1 Check yourself

Once you have taken out the areas you know you aren't feeling, the next step to getting closer to figuring out what you are going to pursue career-wise. Have a look at your strengths, your weaknesses, and the opportunities around you.

TIP

If you want a fresh perspective you could always take a career personality test just to give you some ideas or open your eyes up to new careers or industries you haven't had exposure to yet. These tests give suggestions or indications of what areas you could follow. Don't feel like the results of these tests are final. If they aren't helpful, don't use them.

2 Ask around

If you are still trying to narrow down your focus, ask friends and family what they think would be good for you, or what careers on your list they think you should pursue. The people around you know your personality and will have a genuine idea of what might work for you. You don't have to follow their recommendations, but they might be able to help you pick a path that is right for you. It might also help just to talk through what you have on your mind map with another person, just to help you understand your choices.

3 Do your research

If you can't see a clear career path from what is on your mind map, do some research about what industries or career roles suit your interests. If you aren't sure where to start, a simple Google search can introduce you to new industries you didn't even know existed. There are some amazing organisations dedicated to help you reach your full potential – I have listed some at the end of this chapter.

If you have access to a careers advisor, make time to speak to them. They can give lots of helpful information about the different choices available to you and about how to pursue them. If there isn't anybody locally, you can arrange for a careers advisor from the National Careers Service to schedule a time to call and advise you.

4 Stay schemin'

Once you have an idea of what you want your career to be, you need a **plan** and you need clear and tangible goals to make sure you get there. A plan helps you focus, but can also inspire and motivate you. When you focus on where you are going to end up, you get less upset about the small, day-to-day failures. A plan also reminds you why you are making sacrifices. As always, you need to be flexible with your plan and use it as a guide, not a rule book.

'Plan a roadmap for the future.'
Sharmadean Reid [3]

Dig deep

Claudine Adeyemi, founder and CEO
of the Career Ear

Give yourself the time and space to dig deep and think. I brainstorm with a piece of paper and pen – old school. What are your interests? What skills do you have, and which of those skills do you enjoy using? What kind of impact do you want to have in your career? What kind of lifestyle do you want? Thinking about things like these will give you a good basis for exploring which career paths could be an option for you. Then, create opportunities to explore your options in more depth – perhaps through work experience, a shadowing opportunity or just through conversation.

The chances of you starting out in the same career that you end up in are slim. There's an increasing expectation that we'll try different things – this will equip us with a range of skills, many of which are transferable, and will enable us to make better informed choices about the career that's right for us. We have a lot of time to play with in our lives when it comes to our career, so try not to pressure yourself into making a decision. And, once you have made a decision, don't worry too much if you later wish to try something new.

Deciding what's right for you

Vanessa Sanyauke,
CEO of Girls Talk London

1 It is really important that you try and quieten outside noise when deciding which subjects to take, and this includes from your teachers, friends and even parents! Think about which subjects you enjoy but are also really good at – and in which you are likely to get the best grades possible.

2 If you know which sector or job you would like to eventually work in, try to do some research to see whether applicants are required to have any special requirements, such as for you to have taken certain subjects.

3 It's a great idea to build up work experience. The first point of call would be to ask your family and even your friends if they have any contacts who may work in the company or sector that you want to get experience in. Think local as well – a lot of people aim for big cities and towns, but don't underestimate the value of approaching small businesses in your area who would have the time to nurture you and show you the ropes.

You don't know what the future has in store

Rachael Twumasi-Corson (she/her), co-founder of Afrocenchix, the first British hair-care brand specifically for afro hair

I struggled to choose subjects at school. I wanted to study art and drama, but ended up doing history and business studies instead, with dance after school. I couldn't decide if I wanted to be a doctor, journalist or psychologist.

So, you can guess what choosing my uni course was like. I wrote about eight different personal statements, then scraped them all and put into Asked Jeeves (this was pre-Google, I'm a 90s baby!), 'What do you study if you don't know what you want to do with your life?' Jeeves said: law. Apparently fifty-seven per cent of law graduates went on to do other things, including international human rights journalism. This was on my career list so I took it as a sign!

I didn't think that a year later I'd start a hair care business, and I definitely didn't think that eight years on I'd be pitching my business to celebrities like Ashton Kutcher and Diddy. I've had ups and downs and more jobs than I can count, and sometimes I wish I'd specialised at a younger age – and wonder if I'd be more established in my career if I had. But then I remember that I love my strange career. I get to run an ethical and sustainable business. The lesson is – you don't know what the future has in store. Do what you find interesting and always keep learning!

My ultimate career plan

Start with a motivational quote from someone who inspires you.

Where are you now?

Before you make a start, it's good to look at where you are now, so that you know what progress you need to make. It is also nice to look back and see how much progress you have already made.

What are your career goals?

Your career goals will change over time, so don't be anxious if you haven't set your mind on a specific role as yet. Your main career goal at this point could be just figuring out which careers or industries are interesting to you.

Long-game goals: Think about something you want to achieve over the next few years, such as going to university or getting a job in your chosen career.

Medium-term goals: These are things that you want to achieve in the next three to six months.

Short-term goals: Focus on the things you want to get done in the next month as small steps towards achieving your long or medium-term goals. For instance, if you want to start a blog, a short-term goal could be to buy your domain.

Step-by-step

For each goal, write out two steps you need to take to get there. Try not to place too many obstacles in your way. If your goal is to improve your camera skills, you don't necessarily need to go on a course or buy an expensive camera; one of your steps could be to practise using your phone to take pictures.

MANTRA THAT INSPIRES YOU ....

....

....

WHERE YOU'RE AT..

....

....

YOUR GOALS

	STEP ONE	STEP TWO
LONG-GAME	....	....
	....	....
	....	....
	....	....
	....	....
MEDIUM-TERM	....	....
	....	....
	....	....
	....	....
	....	....
SHORT-TERM	....	....
	....	....
	....	....
	....	....
	....	....

You gon' learn today!

I don't need to tell you how important it is to get the qualifications you need to reach your goals. You need to do your part now and make sure that you build a good foundation for yourself. Focus on getting the best grades you can for the subjects you have picked, even if you know you don't want to go into higher education.

Not all careers require you to pursue formal higher education, but, whatever field you go in to, you will still need to **master the skills of your craft.** For example, if you want to be a comedian you might not need a degree, but you will need to study your routines and learn how to become a good performer. You could also go on a comedy course or spend time going to other comedians' gigs and making notes on their performances to help hone your own.

> If you feel that you need extra support in order to do well in school, make sure you ask for it. Don't struggle in silence or wait too long before you speak up.

In order to master any skill, you need to have the **discipline** to practise, practise, practise. Anything worth having is something worth working towards. I know it's dry to stay home and study, rehearse or practise for hours when you want to be out living your best **life** but being disciplined and earning your stripes is going to ensure you live your best life in the future.

> Set time each day to make sure you have done all of the work you need to do, perhaps as soon as you get home or even by going to the library after school if you can. This way, you get your work done gradually so you don't fall behind and have to do it all at the end.

'To succeed, you need discipline.'
Maloric Blackman [4]

Do your work

When it comes to knowing the right time to start looking at education programmes, putting in course applications or applying for grants, funding or student loans, I suggest you always have your **eye on the ball.** There's nothing worse than seeing an opportunity that's perfect for you and realising you have missed the deadline. Remember to let everyone around you know what you are trying to do – you never know who will see something that could help you, or might put you in touch with someone useful. If it wasn't for my friends helping me on the last night before applications for work placements closed, I doubt I would have even got onto a work placement that year. I got lucky, but it's better to be smart.

So, instead of scrolling on Instagram or talking to friends on the phone for hours (I do the same damn thing all the time), why not spend some time each week researching different roles and understanding what qualifications you may need to be eligible, or what practical experience you can get? There are loads of great websites and organisations giving young Black women the keys to their industries, some of which are listed at the end of this chapter.

> Tip: Set a diary reminder on your phone once a week to do some research into your desired area. Don't pressure yourself to find all the information out at the same time, just Google and see what comes up.

Work it

Getting **experience or** exposure to an industry you want to work in can be tricky, but it isn't impossible. Sometimes it can be down to who you know, but most people get work experience by applying to formal work experience schemes, going to open days or sending emails out to companies asking if they can offer a short work placement.

If I'm honest, you are going to hear 'no' so many more times than you hear 'yes'. It's upsetting when you're rejected over and over again, and even worse when people don't even get back to you to explain why they haven't been able to offer you a place. But keep **persevering.** Stay strong and consistent – remember, if something is for you, it's yours. The right opportunity will reveal itself at the right time, just stay positive.

Take the risk

Life really is about who you know, but just because you haven't been brought up around the perfect contacts in your chosen industry doesn't mean you can't build your own. Seek out people who work in or have experience in the area that you want to get into. Try sending them a DM, an email or a message on LinkedIn. It can be nerve-wracking to do this, but the worst that can happen is someone not responding or saying no.

When reaching out to people, don't focus too strongly on what you can get out of the connection, such as directly asking them for a job or to act as your mentor. You can end up fumbling the ball because you came on too strong. Sometimes, it's better to just to reach out and ask someone questions about what they do, how they got there and if there's any advice they can give you to help you stand out. Once you've got past that point, you could suggest meeting for coffee. Not only is this is a great way to get advice, but it puts you on their radar. If you end up getting a mentor or an opportunity from it, that is a bonus. Build the relationship slowly but surely and think about the long term, hun.

Pay your dues

You need to **put in the work** if you want to see results. If you can find a shortcut (one that is legit and doesn't require you to compromise your values) take it, but nine times out of ten you will need to work hard and be smart to progress. Sometimes, you will need to make sacrifices in order to get the highest grades, or miss fun days out while you are building your portfolio or meeting with your mentor. It feels peak at the time, but it all pays off.

In work placements, you may have to run errands, make coffee or do the photocopying. Yeah, it's boring, but remember everyone had to start from the bottom and do those tasks at one point. If you can put aside your pride so that you can have a better future, **you will be unstoppable.**

Nothing that is worth having will come easily. Make sure you do the work you need to as soon as you can. You won't just walk into an exam and get the best grades if you haven't studied. When we hear people talking about their journeys, we often hear the phrase 'right place at the right time', but if you've done the research and you are ready, you are ten times more likely to be in the right place at the right time.

Day Ones

Don't see people who are shooting for the same goals as you as being competition – especially if they are friends. You are destined for greatness and will Secure the Bag. Being around people who like you and who are working towards their own goals will not only **push** you harder, but also mean you will have genuine people around you who want you to win. There is nothing better than being able to talk to someone who knows how you feel and who can gas you up when you need it.

TIP

Don't worry about what other people are doing. If you have applied for something and you didn't get it but your friend did, don't be upset. You will get the opportunity that is right for you so focus your energy on that. That opportunity is right for them and it's all good, but it doesn't mean that something better isn't waiting for you.

Don't fear failure

It is actually OK to flop, it's OK to fail and it's OK to fall flat on your face. I have flopped more times than I can count. Not getting the job I wanted, not getting the grades I worked for. Some of my flops were so public too, and the shame alone nearly killed me. But I kept going, and you will need to keep going. Most of the time, our flops make us stronger – we learn from them and we grow. Nothing that is yours will be denied to you, but you need to press on. **Get into flopping,** get used to it, and know that it takes some flops before things go right and that is life – each flop is another chapter to your amazing story.

TIP

Make sure you set dates to check in with your career plan so that you can track how you are doing, and see if you are making progress towards your goals over time. Having regular check-ins is also a good way of working out whether some of the goals on your plan need to change.

A plan is a plan only, it isn't a rule book or a blueprint . If you need to change things because they aren't working, change the plan. That's your business – it is only *your* opinion and dreams that matter. Coming up against bumps in the road forces you to **think creatively** – if you have tried things the traditional way and you are struggling to get your start to meet the right people, you can think about what isn't working and try something different.

Say yes

It is great to choose a path and follow it through, but don't feel that you only need to say yes to experiences or opportunities that on paper directly relate to your dream career. Sometimes, opportunities to develop your abilities come from all kinds of different avenues. So if something interesting comes up and it doesn't exactly slot into your career path, before saying no, think about whether you can use this role to develop your confidence, strategising or communication. Just because it isn't directly in your desired area – or isn't part of your plan – don't assume it won't be helpful. If anything, doing something slightly different will help you to **stand out,** or even help you consider where your interests and passions really lie. Say yes to opportunities if they feel right, you never know who you could meet or what further chances you will get.

And finally ... accept no limits

As a Black girl, **ambition is in your bloodline.** Period. We are natural trailblazers. You come from a line of other phenomenal Black women who have opened the doors for you in every field. These are not only celebrities – these Black women can be your mother, your aunties, your teachers or others around you who are trailblazing in their industries. Each of these Black women have shown us and continue to show us that we need to be ready to kick down any barrier, because on many occasions you will be the first Black woman, or the only Black woman, to work in your industry.

When I was doing my legal internships, I was always the only Black girl. I didn't have any other Black girls to talk to, and it was intimidating being the only one in the group. I wasn't the typical corporate lawyer. I didn't dress like or look like the other girls on the internship. They made it clear they didn't value my opinion or expect me to do well, but I knew what I wanted to achieve and I showed up every day and kept working hard until I got my graduate role. I knew what my plan was, so it didn't matter that others were actively trying to put me down because they didn't believe that a young Black girl deserved to have the same profession as them. Anyway, whatever they thought (or still feel) is irrelevant – I am still here, an award-winning lawyer and I am exceeding my own expectations. I didn't need to worry about fitting in or becoming a carbon copy of someone else while at work. **I believe in myself and I am proud to be me.**

There is no set career destination, but there is a journey and it is a personal one. Any decisions that you make about a career or a business need to be good for you at that moment and to make you proud. Don't be distracted about what other people are doing – you need to own your path and own your journey. Period. **You need to always be your biggest cheerleader.** You will need to promote yourself and push yourself, even when no one else understands what you are trying to achieve. The people around you might not understand the application process for your dream role, but you don't have to go it alone. Let your friends and those close to you in on your plans, as, if they are true Squad Goals, they will be there to lend a helping hand where they can.

'You are the designer of your destiny, you are the author of your story.'
Lisa Nichols [5]

ORGANISATIONS TO HELP YOUNG WOMEN WITH THEIR CAREERS

- ★ Girls Talk London
- ★ WCAN
- ★ Career Alchemy
- ★ Stemettes
- ★ Career Analysts
- ★ National Careers Service
- ★ STEM Social

Finding my path

Dr Anne-Marie Imafidon, MBE
CEO of Stemettes

My journey started with wanting to understand the world better by taking things apart, then trying to build them back together. To me, technology and maths are all about making new things that solve problems. So, I've always chosen them for that reason. At the end of primary school, I passed two GCSEs – one in maths and one in ICT. A year later, aged eleven, I did an A-level in computing. By the age of twenty, I'd left Oxford University with a master's in mathematics and computing. While at university, I did various internships and placements, and had a job in technology at an investment bank. After attending a conference on behalf of the company, I learnt about the problem of under-representation of women across technical fields. It's a big problem that'll affect all of us, so I got started working on Stemettes. Eight years on, we've worked with almost 50,000 young women and non-binary folks across the UK and Europe – and I've received an MBE for my leadership. My career path is nowhere near what I ever imagined it would be, and it continues to surprise me every day.

What I wish I'd known growing up

Sara Collins (she/her), author

I wish I'd known that a career as a writer was something I could have pursued seriously. Then I would have started earlier, and I'd never have wasted all those years as a lawyer. In that alternative universe, I'm on my umpteenth novel, and there's a Booker prize on my shelf. In other words, I'm living the life of my literary idol, Bernardine Evaristo!

Dream big

Rt Hon Diane Abbott MP, Labour politician and MP

Looking back to my childhood in the 1960s, the remarkable thing was that there were virtually no British Black women visible in the professions, the media or the public space. Growing up, I never met a British Black female bank clerk, teacher or any British Black female in an authority role. I had relatives in Jamaica who were teachers or in other professions – but I didn't meet them until I was in my twenties. Here in Britain, my parents and their friends and family were in the standard working-class West Indian occupations of the day: nursing, London Transport and factory work. My parents believed in education and wanted the best for me – but it was beyond their wildest imaginings that their daughter would grow up to be the first Black female MP. So, I marvel at how I got it into my head that I could not only go to Cambridge University, but become an MP. I think that part of it was a fearlessness I had – my most precious legacy from my Jamaican ancestors.

Both my parents came from the same village in the hilly Jamaican parish of Clarendon. Those communities in the hills are the descendants of people who had fled there after after the abolition of slavery, because they refused to cut sugar cane for the white man anymore. They preferred to scratch a living, growing yam and keep their pride. And they bequeathed to me the imperishable sense that I was as good as anybody. It also helped that I went to a girls' grammar school. I was the only Black girl there, and I experienced the usual institutional racism, and I certainly wasn't encouraged to apply to Cambridge. But old-fashioned girls' schools taught us that, not only were we as good as boys, but often we were better.

The other thing that set me on my improbable journey to Westminster was that I was a dreamer. In those days, there was no inter net and only two TV channels, and so my dreams were woven around the books that I read. In those books, people went to university and had exciting careers, meaning I formed the view that I could do these things too. I manged to miss the fact that all the people in the novels I read were white.

What I would say to young girls growing up today is to dream big and do not set a limit to your ambitions! Just because you cannot see someone who looks like you in a certain role or profession does not mean that you cannot do it. If the chubby, bespectacled, Black schoolgirl that I was could be become an MP, then literally anything is possible. Only believe.

9 Secure the Bag

Paving the way to live your best life

By Natalie

'**S**ecure the Bag' isn't just a mantra for a year or period of time, it should be the mantra of your entire life! The Bag is anything you want or desire – it could be getting the dream job, starting a business, travelling, obtaining a certain qualification or status, or getting paid what you truly deserve for your work. That's why it is so important to have a **vision** for your life, knowing what you want to achieve and what you stand for. As you go through different experiences in life, your goals and dreams will change, but it's still good to take some time out to think about what success looks like to you now.

We spoke about picking a career and getting qualifications in Chapter 8 but there's so much more to success and fulfilment than getting your dream job, and that's what this chapter is about. You may start off believing that reaching a certain professional goal is you Securing the Bag, but after a few years, you may realise that you want a completely different lifestyle. That can be hard to accept if you have been on one set path for so long.

When I was growing up and contemplating my future, I was only encouraged to think about what job I was going to do. I knew I wanted to be a lawyer and decided from a young age to reach for that goal, but part of me really wanted to be a music journalist, an actress, a cook and a writer too. Although they aren't the career paths I chose, they remained a part of my vision for the future. I never once gave up on my dream to write a book, and look at me now! Sometimes it just takes a little longer, and a slightly different path, to get there.

'Ask for what you want and be prepared to get it.'
Maya Angelou [1]

You can start a new side venture, study something new or pick up a new skill at any time. I started Black Girls' Book Club with Mel while working as a corporate lawyer. Neither of us had the time, but we made it work because we were passionate about reading stories about Black women, and we wanted to share our passion with other Black women. We had **no idea** what we created would grow the way it has, and I didn't know that my love for reading could ever lead to anything – but it did. I'm still focused on my career path in law, but Black Girls' Book Club has **enriched** my life in such a different way. The key is to stay open to all your ambitions and embrace new challenges and opportunities as they arise, because dreams can manifest themselves in ways you might have never imagined.

And remember, you don't need to neatly fit into any category or knock on any doors for permission.

With all the decisions you are being asked to make about your future, it can seem like you have to make all the important choices so early on, but that really isn't the case. Don't ever feel bad because you don't know what you want to be doing in twenty years' time – it's normal to feel that way, and not knowing gives you an opportunity to really explore. You need to take time to identify your goals, figure out your passions and what you really love. **Be patient** with yourself and don't listen to what others say. You need to do things in your own time, when you are ready and once you know what your vision for your life is. The seasoning tastes best when its left overnight to marinate.

I am always inspired by stories about Black women. Ava DuVernay, an award-winning director, didn't pick up a camera until she was in her thirties and had a whole different career in journalism, marketing and PR before she became the world-renowned filmmaker we know today.

As a young Black girl, people may purposefully put barriers in your way, or overlook you in favour of others who aren't half as talented – but don't ever be discouraged. You will not always have the privileges other people have had. Maybe you didn't go to the best school or have parents with connections, but so what? Focus on your plans, your goals and Securing your Bag. It takes a lot to throw you off focus when you believe in yourself and you know what you are here to do. Regardless of what bad mind people try and do, you can literally destroy any barrier anyone places before you. You've just got to stay scheming, and I'm going to give you some ideas for how to do just that.

Know yourself

You may be reading this and worrying that you have no idea what your Bag is, or how to figure it out. One of the best ways to work out what you want for your life is to really **get to know yourself.**

Knowing who you are is an ongoing process. Even at my big big age I am still figuring it out. Ultimately, you have to spend time with yourself. You, and only you. Think about what makes you happy, the things you like about your life right now and what you feel your purpose is. Spend time doing the things you like to do, and take time away from others and social media just to be in **your own space.** It's hard to **hear your inner voice** when there is so much going on around you. I know if you have a big family or don't have much physical space to call your own this can be tough, but it is important that you give time to your own thoughts – whether that means going for walks by yourself, mediating, taking yourself out for meals or trips alone.

Keep a notebook and pen with you, and write about the first thing that comes to your mind. It could be a word or a sentence but keep doing this daily and watch and see what happens!

Another good way to get to know yourself is to journal regularly. It is such an easy way to get things off your chest in a safe space, and you can be honest about how you feel about your life, the people around you and any other things that may be on your mind. Journaling doesn't have to take a long time, it can be five minutes you give yourself each day as soon as you wake up, or just before you go to bed. You will be surprised how many ideas will naturally flow once you give yourself five minutes on your own to clear your mind.

> **TIP**
> *If you can't seem to shake your fears, write them out on a piece of paper. Once done, fold the paper into the smallest piece possible and then throw it away. Once the fears are out of your system, write down everything that could go right and what would actually happen if you pushed through.*

Be fearless

There is no one else like you. Fact. **You are a one-time, one-off, custom-designed exclusive.** Don't ever approach any aspect of your life with fear. When you are taking the time to think about what you want and what is important for you, don't change your mind because something seems too far out of your reach, or impossible for you to achieve. **There is nothing you cannot achieve:** like I said in Chapter 8, if it's meant for you, it's yours. If you know a certain lifestyle is for you, own it. If your plan is to impact others in a powerful way, commit to it. These dreams are yours for a reason.

'You are your best thing.'
Toni Morrison [2]

I spent so many of my teenage years being so fearful or worried about what others would say about my goals, or what would happen if something didn't work out. I let these people (who I don't even chat to or care about now) have so much power over my choices, and for what? You owe it to yourself to **believe** in your sauce and to take risks. This is your life and it's too short for you to be fighting against yourself. You have to be brave. You betting on yourself and taking that year out to travel on your own could be the best thing you ever do, and may open so many doors for you. You writing that script and recording that short film on your phone could be the start of a phenomenal journey as a director. Make the leap or you'll never know.

Go for it

Jamelia Donaldson, founder and CEO of TreasureTress, Europe's first and largest natural hair product subscription box

My courage to launch TreasureTress was the result of pure naivety. I had no business experience, nothing to lose and I wouldn't have it any other way. If I had weighed up everything that could've gone wrong – such as trading in my high-paying corporate career to launch 'an experiment' – I probably wouldn't have ever started. But my curiosity got the best of me – I wanted to see what would happen if for the first time in my life I gave something 100% of my attention and effort. What would happen if I truly 'went for it'? No-one has all of the answers and, like most things in life, there are no guarantees. Deciding to simply 'go for it' is just about making one decision, and then being disciplined and committed to showing up every single day.

Be open

If you aren't sure what is for you or what your path will be just yet, be open. To new opportunities, new perspectives, new foods, different cultures – be open to everything. You never know where your life will take you, so don't start cutting yourself off from what this world has to offer because it doesn't fit in with what's immediately around you. Something may look like it isn't for you at first, but you can **give it a try** and if you don't like it you are just one step closer to finding out what is best for you. You may want to travel to a new place on your own, or try to create a new piece of art - whatever opportunity comes your way, if you feel it, try it. Most people figure out what they like by trying new experiences and making the best out of the worst circumstances.

You can learn skills from unexpected places that can be applied to so many different areas of your life. Jackie Aina was in the military for years before she became a global beauty influencer. She worked on perfecting her craft, creating videos while she was still serving, and she says being in the military taught her a lot about gratitude, leadership and perseverance. Who would have thought that a soldier would end up as one of the most prominent and outspoken Black make-up influencers in the world? Everything is a learning experience, and sometimes we take the longer path because we need to grow to get to a point where we can fully reap and sustain the benefits of our success.

Be bold

Bolanle Tajudeen,
founder and CEO of Black Blossoms

Before I have to publicly launch a business project, my belly gets twists and aches, I can feel the palms of my hands become sweaty and my entire body wants to find somewhere to hide. I'm overthinking about how the world will receive my project, whether anyone will care, and what happens if it fails. In all the instances I have felt like this, I have had to be bold, feel the fear and proceed anyway. Fear is a natural reaction to starting and sharing something new, but hiding your talents from the world is unnatural. The truth is on the other side of fear you have so many people rooting for you and wanting to help you reach the next level of your self-defined destiny. Be bold and blossom.

Be creative

When we think about what we want for our lives, we might not always be able to see a pathway there. Sometimes, we just wish that the path **to our happiest life** could be clear and straight-forward, but it usually isn't. There will be moments when you feel like you have taken ten steps forwards, and then, in a second, something has flopped and you are back where you started. But just because you can't see exactly how something is going to work out, it doesn't mean that it isn't right for you.

'Never be afraid to sit awhile and think.'
Lorraine Hansberry [3]

This is where we need to **think differently.** You don't have to do anything in the 'traditional' way. You can create your own lane, your own space and your own opportunities. You may not be able to plot out a step-by-step plan of how you will get something, but do not be worried because you will figure things out. The main thing is to **be bold** and take some sort of action towards your dreams – they won't come true on their own. I always say, I would rather ask for forgiveness than ask for permission.

As a young Black woman, you will face so many more obstacles and the answers will not come easily. Remember, you come from a long line of trailblazing and creative Black women who have consistently created opportunities for themselves. If a solution is not coming to you easily - talk to your friends or meditate it on it and an answer will come to you – trust the process. Don't give up because someone has told you 'no', or that it can't be done – there is always a way.

Don't be afraid to ignore what people say. I really struggle when it comes to making decisions, and so I used to go around and ask everyone for their opinion. But I had to realise that not everyone had my best interests at heart, or they thought that they knew me better than I knew myself and told me to limit my expectations. Deep down, you know what feels right – trust your instinct, always.

'I thrive on obstacles. If I'm told that it can't be, then I push harder.'
Issa Rae [4]

Be patient

We are so used to having everything come to us quickly that it can be hard when we have to wait for the results of our hard work to make an appearance. We might even have to start from scratch when we have gone down the wrong path, we you shouldn't be too hard on ourselves if our plans aren't working out.

There have been many times in my life where I have had to **start again** and, while it was hard at the time and I felt embarrassed or sad, starting again has always been the best thing for me. You might be convinced that you have found your vision and purpose, pursue it with all your effort and sacrifice only to realise half way through that you are on the completely wrong path. You may decide that you really want to live abroad, then move to your dream location and hate it and want to come back. It may feel like you've failed and, even worse, look like failure to everyone around you, but you will continue to change as you grow and you need to be patient with yourself. You aren't going to wake up one day as the perfect 7.0 version of yourself – every day and every new experience is part of your upgrading process. Fall in love with this process, as it never stops. The more you embrace it, the more empowering it will be. Don't be in a rush for anything – it all happens at the appointed time. There is no perfect age or time by which you need to have achieved all your goals.

Dream out loud

What you think and say about yourself, and to yourself, is so important. Our words are powerful and can change everything in our lives. If you believe something is for you, say it – and then say it **again and again and again.** The more you speak positively about your life and your future, the better your mindset will be. These positive statements which are personal to you are **affirmations.** I say positive things to and about myself daily. This isn't me having a big ego – it is me affirming who I am, and you should do the same. Saying affirmations daily can help build your confidence and keep you aligned to your purpose. They can also help you **remain calm** in times of stress and help you combat negative feelings and thought processes you may be having. Making positive affirmations can also encourage you to be open to opportunities, and creative and consistent in your efforts to live your very best life.

Your affirmations

Each day, try telling yourself things you need to hear in order to restore your confidence, and set yourself up with the mindset to conquer the things that are frightening you or making you anxious. Write down three things you need to believe about yourself below and repeat them daily or as many times as you need to. For me, my current daily affirmations are: I am a creative person, I solve problems and I believe in myself. I keep these in my phone, on stickie notes on my desk and on the front of notebooks as a constant reminder.

.... 's daily affirmations

....

....

....

....

Affirmations can change all the time, so feel free to remix them or take inspiration from mine just to get you going. You can even record voice notes and play them to yourself each morning or throughout the day when you need a reminder of how truly amazing you are.

When creating my vision board, I looked at a lot of old magazines and cut out pictures. I also printed things that I had screenshotted on my phone from social media. I didn't just include pictures of objects, I printed off pictures of women who inspired me as well. I included a photo of Lydie, one of my closest friends who had moved away, because I wanted her to remain one of my best friends and she still is till this day. Your vision board can include anything that is important to you.

Create your vision board

Once you've figured out what you want, you need to get it down on paper. One of the best ways to do this is to create a vision board. Having a vision board that you can look at every day helps you **to stay focused on your goals.**

There are **no rules** about what you put on your vision board, you can include anything that you want to achieve, as well as things that motivate and inspire you. It doesn't have to relate to career or education goals only. It can have anything on it – a pair of shoes, a restaurant you want to try, a holiday or an experience you're working towards. If you know you want to be an award-winning film director, for example, you can include a picture of the award you are going to win on your board. You can include an event that has already happened if you want to achieve something again, or a trinket that reminds you of when you felt great. When you are selecting things to put on your vision board, don't hold back. Put down exactly what you want, even if it seems impossible. Don't worry about covering every inch of the board – I always try to leave space just in case I want to add something new to it later on.

Creating a vision board is simple. Just take images, handwritten notes, goals and quotes that inspire you or relate to what you want in life, then arrange them on the card in any way you want. Once you have finished, put the board up where you can see it every day. And remember, there are many other ways to create vision boards if you can't physically make one. You can create a virtual mood board by copying and pasting your images onto a Word document, or you can use Instagram or Pinterest to store images, videos or inspirational quotes that you want to apply to your life.

.... 'S VISION BOARD LIST:

- A big piece of card (A3 recommended)
- Glue or Sellotape or pins

- Space to put the vision board up once it's done
- A free hour (or two)
- No TV or phone
- Photos
- Inspirational quotes

- Handwritten goals
- Trinkets

Story time

I love shoes, they are my first and only true love! I once saw a pair of shoes worn by an influencer on Instagram and I knew one day I would have them – but they were so expensive and I couldn't justify spending that money as I was trying to move out of my parents' house at the time. I printed off the picture of the shoes from Instagram and put them on my vision board. Months later, I'd completely forgotten about the shoes and was on my way to a festival abroad. As I was walking around the duty-free shops in Berlin Airport, I saw the shoes – seventy per cent off the original price and, imagine, the only size left in the entire store was my size! Every day for the last seven months before that moment, I had seen the shoes on my vision board. I had seen them so many times that I took them for granted, and yet I got them when I least expected it at a price I could afford. After that day, anything I wanted (more shoes, yes, but not just shoes) I printed off and put it on my vision board – and everything I wanted started happening when I least expected it.

Your flavour

Creating a vision for your life is the **most important** thing you can do for yourself. Once you know what you are trying to achieve and know what you deserve, it will shape how you approach your entire life. This is a process, and you should see success as your secret recipe for your very best dish – there may be some overall principles as to how you make a particular dish, but everyone has their different ways, secret ingredients and special techniques when it comes to making their version. Remember, you define what success looks like to you, and if that means you have to forge a new path and do something that no one else is trying to do, so be it. Securing the Bag is about you securing the best future for yourself and **living your very best life,** on your terms.

Prioritise yourself

Liv Little (she/her), award-winning writer, consultant, creative director and curator, and the founder of *gal-dem* - a media company that spotlights the creative talents of women and non-binary people of colour

Prioritise your well-being just as much as you prioritise work and relationships. You are the most precious thing and caring for yourself is an ongoing process. Remember, you don't have to be the version of yourself that you think other people want to see, you are great as you are and you have so much to contribute to this planet. Look after and love yourself, stay curious and keep learning. Nothing is fixed forever. Embracing change and investing in possibility will be your best friend.

You are enough

Audrey Indome,
co-host of The Receipts podcast

To the little sisters who'll read this book, I'm here to pass on a message that I can only wish someone had been able to give to me when I was younger. You are enough. The world will try and tell you otherwise, but anytime they do, just remember it's your features they want, it's your skin they want, it's your natural sauce they want. You won't get the credit you deserve but that's OK – what's understood doesn't need to be explained. I think my calling is to let young women know that society will try and confine them to a box based on age. But, as someone who found success in her thirties, I can say it's a myth. I was thirty when the podcast started, and I believe that without life experience I wouldn't be able to bring the magic I do to the show. It's never too late to follow your dreams.

Be kind to yourself

Afua Hirsch (she/her), broadcaster,
writer and bestselling author

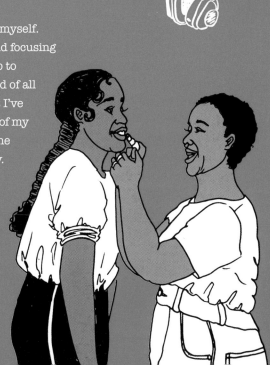

Growing up, I wish I had been kinder to myself. I was so busy being critical of myself, and focusing on what I wanted to be, that I didn't stop to appreciate what I already was. I'm proud of all the things I've done – even the mistakes I've made have been such an important part of my journey. I just wish I had taken more time for gratitude and self-love along the way.

10 Money moves

Part 1

Finessing your finances
How to budget

By Natalie

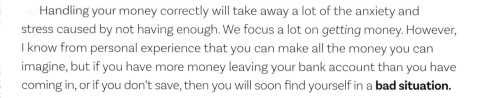

Taking care of your finances is a big part of growing up and showing out. Financial independence is the key to living your best life.

Handling your money correctly will take away a lot of the anxiety and stress caused by not having enough. We focus a lot on *getting* money. However, I know from personal experience that you can make all the money you can imagine, but if you have more money leaving your bank account than you have coming in, or if you don't save, then you will soon find yourself in a **bad situation.**

When I was younger, I had to rely on the set amount of money my parents gave me each week. I had to make sure my lunch money stretched Monday to Friday, and that my pocket money lasted for the whole weekend. I thought my dad was being mean at the time, but actually he was trying to teach me to treat money with respect, and show me that I would need to work to get the things I really wanted. I used to see my friends spending money on clothes, hair and going to Nando's, and I thought that if I just earned my own money, I could buy everything I wanted. So, I got a weekend job. I thought things would get easier as soon as I started working, but having more money didn't solve my problems. As I got the money, I spent it – and I ended up broke waiting for my next pay cheque. I soon learnt that if I wanted something, I needed to **put in that work** to get it for myself.

You may think you are too young to start learning about how to look after money because your parents are taking care of you and you don't have a job or any bills yet. But TRUST ME, **managing money is a key life skill**. So many of the financial mistakes I made in the past were because I didn't know any better. Learning how to look after your finances is a major part of self-care. Educating yourself about money and how to use it is just as important as getting the best grades or looking after your mental health.

Now, I don't want you to be obsessed or uptight about money, but I also don't want you to be stressed or suffer with anxiety because you don't have enough. You should never be ashamed about not having enough money or have to worry about it. So, in this chapter Mel and I are here to show you how to make the best out of what you have, and how to start planning ahead so that you don't have to go without.

Budget over everything

If you don't want to be in a position where you are constantly overspending or spending money on the wrong things, you need a BUDGET.

I don't remember ever thinking about setting a budget when I first started working. I just spent the money and expected more to follow because I knew I was going to work the next week. I kept up with this way into my early adult life. I wasted a lot of money, ran up more **debts** and **bills** than I needed to, all because I didn't organise my finances properly. Every time I ran into a financial issue, I just thought about how I could make more money to fix it. Instead of grinding, what I really needed to learn was **how to say no** to going out with friends or buying clothes or make-up, especially when I had other important things to pay for.

I'm going to give you a quick step-by-step of how to write a budget. I've also created template for you to fill in. One type of budget isn't going to work for everyone – and at different points in your life your budget will change – but hopefully this will help you get started. So, let's get into it.

1 How much money do you have?
AKA cash is QUEEN

Is your budget based on money given to you by your parents? Is it money from your weekend job or from you providing a service (for example, doing someone's hair)? Or is it a one-off amount, like a birthday present? Will you get the same amount again next week or next month or next year?

Write that amount of money at the top of your budget.

If your money is predictable (for example, if you get paid every month) it makes sense to have a budget that is fixed on a period of time. However, if your money is more random it might be better to write a simple budget each time you get a sum of money so that you can plan what you want to spend it on and **don't waste it.** For example, you could have a budget setting out how you are going to spend your birthday money.

You might also want to have a **budget** if you are given money to spend on a school trip or on a holiday. If you want to work out how much money you should be spending in a day when you are on holiday, divide your holiday money by the number of days you are away. For example, if you have £200 and you're away for four days, that gives you £50 to spend each day. You don't have to spend all of your daily allowance though – if you have anything left over you can always bring it home and use that money for something else.

2 What do you need to spend your money on?
AKA bills, bills, bills

You need to have a real understanding of what you actually need to spend your money on if you want your budget to work. These are called your **expenses.** If you don't include these in your budget, you will fall short on money faster than you expected. The best budgets include as many of your expenses as possible. So, write a list of everything you might need to spend money on in a month. This could include money for the school bus, food, books or even essential items, such as beauty products.

Work out the total amount of money needed for your expenses and put that in your budget.

Remember, your budget should be realistic. If you know that you usually spend £5 a day on lunch, don't budget for £3 a day. If you need to make cuts that is fine, but always make sure these cuts are sensible. If you cut back too much, you will end up overspending and be back at square one!

3 How much money is left over? AKA extra credit

CASH IS QUEEN - BILLS BILLS BILLS = EXTRA CREDIT

What figure are you left with? Is it positive or negative? This is the amount of money you have left over for the next two steps.

4 Savings AKA racks on racks

Regularly saving money is one of the best habits you can develop. You never know what's coming around the corner so it's always good to have money set aside for your future. You don't have to be saving for something big, such as a holiday or a designer handbag, it's best just to have a pot of money that you can rely on for **unexpected costs.**

You should try and take savings out of your spending money as soon as you can. This ensures you are building up your pot every time you get some cash. It doesn't have to be a lot – it could be something as small as £1. If you stay consistent, putting aside small amounts on a regular basis, it will make a BIG difference after a while.

You never know when it will come in handy. You might decide at the last minute to take a year out after school and travel – your savings could cover your flights or accommodation. You could use it to start your own business, or put it towards your living expenses if you move out for uni. It could go towards your first car or even your first home. The point is, having that money gives you choices and freedom to do things you wouldn't be able to without it.

5 What do you want to spend your money on? AKA treat yourself

Now, write a list of things you would like to spend your money on - for example, going out with your friends or buying anything you want.

Add these things to your budget.

Budget template

Now, try following these steps using the template below. I'd suggest starting with a monthly budget, then you can work up to a yearly- or longer-term budget when you're ready.

.... 'S BUDGET

DATE: ....

Step 1: CASH IS QUEEN (money in):

Before you make a start, it's good to look at where you are now, so that you know what progress you need to make. It is also nice to look back and see how much progress you have already made.

JOB: £ ....

ALLOWANCE: £ ....

ONE-OFF AMOUNTS: £ ....

TOTAL IN: £ ....

Step 2: BILLS, BILLS, BILLS (important expenses):

1. ....

2. ....

3. ....

4. ....

TOTAL EXPENSES: £ ....

Step 3: EXTRA CREDIT (money left over)

CASH IS QUEEN – BILLS BILLS BILLS
= EXTRA CREDIT: £ ....

Step 4: SAVINGS

MONEY TO ADD TO LONG-TERM SAVINGS: £ ....

MONEY TO ADD TO SHORT-TERM SAVINGS : £ ....

THINGS YOU ARE SAVING FOR IN THE SHORT TERM
(FOR EXAMPLE, HOLIDAY MONEY): ....

EXTRA CREDIT – SAVINGS = SPENDING MONEY: £ ....

Step 5: SPENDING MONEY (what you want to spend your money on now): (Tip: Make sure you include the cost of each thing.)

1. ....

2. ....

3. ....

4. ....

MONEY LEFT OVER (IF ANY): £ ....

Now you have written a budget, you know how much you have to spend for a certain amount of time. You also know what your most important expenses are. By budgeting, you may realise that you can't afford to get everything at once, and might need to put some money aside so that you can buy those extras later. Ultimately, if you don't have the money for it, don't spend it. Don't get sucked in to going out or buying expensive things you can't afford because everyone else around you is doing the same – there's rice at home and there's always next time.

Part 2

Know your worth
Financial literacy

By Melissa

Cardi B talking about 'making money moves' isn't just a hot line in an even hotter song. Making money moves, or smart and informed financial decisions, will not only assist you with Securing the Bag, but will also go a long way to helping you secure the future that you want. You may feel like you're too young to make serious financial choices – but with things coming up such as starting university or an apprenticeship, taking a gap year or even getting your first job, you are at a critical point in your life, and it makes sense to get a head start. Part of that is taking the time to gain a good understanding of financial terms and processes so you have a **strong foundation** of knowledge for the future.

'If you're going to play the game properly, you'd better know every rule.'
Barbara Jordan [1]

While it isn't widely taught in schools, financial literacy is as vital as learning to read and write. Understanding the way money works allows you to effectively navigate life and avoid traps - such as soaring debt, high interest rates, banking fraud and a crippling overdraft. Just like having good grades or learning something new, working on your financial literacy is a beneficial and achievable way of ensuring that you develop a **toolkit of skills** that will help you on your journey to becoming grown.

Throughout this book you will have noticed that Natalie and I put a big emphasis on determining your own destiny. There is a strength and power that develops when you're able to use your skills, passions and the help of others to take control of your life choices. Understanding how money works is a big part of that.

'I have a passion for music, I love music. But I also have a passion for money and paying my bills.'
Cardi B [2]

No one is born knowing how to handle money – it's something that is passed down by elders, and learned through experience. Some of us may have had family members and friends who, perhaps for reasons outside of their control, haven't been the best examples of healthy financial management. This intergenerational cycle can make financial independence and social mobility difficult to achieve. But, by taking an interest in money management now and planning for the future, you'll be well on your way to financial freedom – ensuring you always stay ready. Let's get into it.

Money isn't everything

You may have heard the phrase, 'money makes the world go round'. Or, if your parents are anything like mine, 'money doesn't grow on trees'. It can often seem like everyone is always talking about money, but it's really important that before we dig any deeper into this chapter, I make it abundantly clear that money **isn't** everything. I can't deny that having the latest phone, new trainers or even the best 613 hair can make you feel on top of the world. But your mental health and overall wellbeing are worth more than anything money can buy. Let me be clear: the **amount of money you have doesn't define the type of person you are.** You may be in a position where there are economic differences between yourself and your friends. It could be that some of the tips that I provide may not be something you are able to try right now. That's perfectly fine.

Money doesn't make you – your personal worth is not tied up in how much money you or your family has, and you should never think you are better than someone else because you have more money than them.

'I let money serve its purpose. But I don't live to serve money.'
Oprah Winfrey [3]

Family advice

Personally, I've always had a good relationship with money. My mum made a conscious effort to show me her credit card statements, bills and payslips, taking time to explain to me what everything meant. She would even ask me to go into the bank on her behalf to pay utility bills. At the time, I didn't really understand the necessity or even the importance of what she was doing. But it meant that when I got my first job, I was able to easily **navigate** things such as taking out a mobile phone contract and setting up a direct debit, as well as putting aside some money to pay for nights out with my friends.

However, the fact that I was lucky enough to have a basic understanding of how things like cash and credit worked didn't stop me running up bills on my very first credit card. As my aunties would say, 'Those who cannot hear, must feel' – and I very quickly learned that having a big credit limit means nothing if you aren't able to pay back your minimum payment.

Now, this isn't an excuse to ask your family members how much money they have in the bank! But you can ask for real-life examples in order to supplement the knowledge you are gaining about financial literacy in *Grown*.

Often, money can be the biggest conversational taboo. People will tell you what they had for dinner last night, add you to their 'close friends' on Instagram and reveal their deepest and darkest secrets. But ask them how much money they have in the bank – or even the sacrifices they have made to buy the things they have – and they start stuttering. While for some people, money is no object – budget isn't even in their vocabulary.

Budget? I don't know her.

Mo' money mo' problems: A dictionary of terms

Being **financially secure** is more than having stacks of money in the bank. It's understanding how money works and putting steps in place for money to work for you. Nat's already talked about budgeting, and so I want to continue by breaking down some of the other financial terms you may have heard.

Quick terms to know

Credit limit: This is the maximum amount of money your bank will lend you to spend on an overdraft or credit card.

Credit rating/score: In simple terms, your credit score is a collection of data that tells potential lenders your financial history. It **predicts** your future spending habits based on the way you have behaved in the past. It includes information such as any money you may owe, previous credit products you have used or loans you have taken out, as well as any recent credit applications you may have made. It also records whether you pay on time.

This essentially allows lenders to decide whether they should take a financial risk on you. A good credit rating means you're more likely to be accepted for products such as phone contracts, loans or 'buy now, pay later' schemes. Poor credit can end up excluding you from these things or even penalising you – if companies see you as financially unreliable, they may increase the amount of interest they charge when lending you money, as there is a higher risk that you won't be in a position to pay them back.

Direct debit: An arrangement made with your bank to allow a third party, such as a mobile phone company, to transfer money from your account to pay your bills on an agreed date.

Financial Conduct Authority (FCA): The FCA regulates the financial services in the UK and aims to protect us, the consumers. Through their Financial Services Compensation Scheme, the FCA guarantees protection of money deposited with a bank, building society or credit union up to a limit of £85,000 – so you won't lose it even if the bank were to collapse.

Interest: As an incentive to 'hold' or look after the money in your current or savings account, the bank pays you an additional percentage of the total amount – this is called **interest.** In simple terms, the money you have saved earns its own money.

This also works the other way, as interest can also be charged to you. If you borrow money or use a 'buy now, pay later' scheme, you may be charged an additional percentage on top of the borrowed amount. It's essentially an extra fee charged to you for the privilege of being able to use money you would usually not have access to.

Minimum payment: This is the minimum amount you must pay towards an outstanding balance you owe. For example, on a credit card there will be a fixed minimum amount for you to repay each month.

Payslip: These are statements that show how much you have been paid over a set period of time. Your payslip will show your rate of pay, how much you've earned overall, your tax code and any deductions made for things like tax, your pension and paying off your student loan.

Tax: This is a compulsory charge that the government asks its citizens to pay in order to fund public services, such as schools, the NHS and local parks. Tax is collected when you have a job and you earn a salary.

> 'You wanna know how rich
> people like me stay rich?
> By staying on a budget.'
> **Cardi B** [4]

What's in a word?
Your financial cheat sheet

What follows are the key terms you need to know in relation to looking after your money, borrowing and saving. This list is just a start – if you come across any financial terms that you're unsure about or if you want to learn more, you can talk to someone at your bank or local Citizens Advice.

Current account
What is it? A personal account that you can put money into when you want to save, and take out whenever you need it. Think of it as a piggy bank with extra security.

Overdraft
What is it? An overdraft is a form of borrowing from the bank. Essentially, you can 'overdraw' an amount of money that is more than the amount of cash in your account.

What do you need to know? There are two types of overdraft.

• **Arranged overdraft:** Where the bank permits you to spend more money than is currently in your account, by giving you an additional figure you can spend up to.

• **Unarranged overdraft:** Where you have spent more money than is in your current account without the bank's permission. This could be because you haven't agreed an overdraft limit or you have exceeded your existing overdraft limit.

Remember, overdrafts are a type of loan and should only be used if you can **guarantee** you can pay it back. Banks will always take any money in your account to cover your overdraft. That means if you are overdrawn, any money that comes into your account will cover your debts first.

Credit card

What is it? Effectively this little piece of plastic lets you spend money to your heart's content. **On credit.** It's a loan given to you by your card provider that allows you to spend up to a set limit, which you then must pay back within a set amount of time. The amount you are able to spend is dependent on whether your card provider believes you have the ability to pay it back on time.

What do you need to know? Credit isn't bad, as long as you know how to manage it. It's always in your best interest to pay off more than the minimum required payment each month, and, ideally, the full amount you owe if you can. Doing so ensures that you won't pay interest on what you've borrowed. Plus, credit cards are **safer than cash** – as you're protected for most purchases over £100 and up to £30,000, which means if something goes wrong, you can get your money back.

Remember: Section 75 of the Consumer Credit Act allows you to make a claim against your credit card company to get your money back.

Story time

I once flew all the way to Amsterdam to see Drake in concert, but as we were getting ready to go to the show we found out he was still in the USA with J Lo! (Allegedly.) That was it. The concert was cancelled with barely any notice. I was big mad. Not only had I spent the best part of the evening getting ready. Sending snaps. Letting people know I was in Amsterdam having the time of my life. I had spent a lot of money on the ticket. However, when I phoned the venue, they refused to refund me. I was vexed! I thought I had lost my money. Until I remembered I paid for the tickets with my credit card. I called my credit card company with the quickness and quoted Section 75 of the Consumer Credit Act, and every penny of the ticket cost was returned.

TIP

Setting up a direct debit for the minimum payment (so the money automatically leaves your current account) means you will never miss a credit card bill. Missed payments can negatively impact your credit rating and lead to extra charges.

Credit cards have some downsides too. The bottom line is, you need to make at least the minimum payment on your credit card each month. Even if you have an interest-free period. Making a cash withdrawal with your credit card is a no-no. It can negatively impact your credit rating because it suggests that you have **no money** in your current account. In addition to this, there are usually harsh financial penalties attached to withdrawing money from your credit card, such as a higher interest rate being charged.

Charge card

What is it? Charge cards are NOT to be confused with credit cards. Yes, you can use them to buy something now and pay for it later – but the big difference is that you have to pay it off in full every month.

What do you need to know? Often, charge cards have super high spending limits. Or, if you've got it like that, there may be no spending limit at all.

What do you need to watch out for? Unlike a credit card, you don't have the benefit of running up a big bill and paying it back at your convenience. Not repaying in full at the end of the month can leave you with big penalties, such as additional interest.

'Buy now, pay later'

What is it? Pay later options effectively allow you to delay making immediate payment when you're purchasing an item. Payments can be delayed from fourteen days later to twelve months or more, depending on the retailer. These schemes are often available when you're buying things online like trainers and clothes, and even expensive items such as laptops and phones.

What do you need to know? Now, this option appears to come with a lot of perks - you can buy what you want without spending a penny. Who wouldn't want to get the perfect outfit without having to break the bank? But remember, there are consequences - and you will have to pay back what you spent, if not more, at some point - often this can be as much 45 per cent more.

Example

To put this into perspective, let's do some quick maths. Say you purchase a pair of Nike VaporMax 360s from a popular online fashion retailer on 1 January. They cost £180. You decide to use the 'buy now, pay later' scheme – allowing you to defer payments for 12 months with an interest rate of 45% per year. You wear your trainers for a few months, forget about them and throw them under the bed. The following January, it's time to pay up. And you now owe that online retailer £261. Yes, you read that right. Two hundred and sixty-one English pounds! You end up paying nearly double for the privilege of using the service.

Now, there are benefits to using the 'buy now, pay later' system, and you can navigate it to ensure that you don't pay much interest. Or even any at all. Every scheme is different, but, using my trainer story opposite, I've made a note of three scenarios below that you can use to ensure you don't get finessed.

• Divide the amount owed by 12. You can then pay £15 a month – from the month the trainers are ordered. Ensuring that not only are they paid for in full during the year, but that you also avoid paying any interest.

• You can pay for the trainers in full with one lump sum at any point during the twelve-month period. Again, avoiding paying any interest.

• You can pay a portion of the amount owed, let's say £90, during the twelve-month period. You end up paying interest on whatever amount is left: in this case you would end up paying another £130 at the end of the twelve-month period, with £50 of that figure amounting to interest.

Mobile phone contract

What is it? A monthly fee, fixed for a set period of time and paid to a mobile phone network in exchange for a mobile phone and/or services such as minutes and data.

What do you need to know? If your contract includes a phone rather than just a sim card, technically you don't own that phone until the contract is paid off. Contracts give you the opportunity to own an expensive handset without the upfront cost. However, phone contracts, like any other financial agreement, often benefit the provider more than the customer. You will find that over the course of your contract you end up spending more than you would have done if you had bought the phone outright. But not everyone has £900+ spare to buy a phone!

Loan

What is it? A loan is an exchange of money with the promise that it will be paid back over an agreed time period.

What do you need to know? Similar to credit, the amount you can borrow in the form of a loan is dependent on what a bank thinks you will be able to pay back. Loans can be taken out for everything, from starting your own business to purchasing a home, this is called a mortgage). If you are taking a loan from a financial institution like a bank, they will often impose an amount of interest on the sum you request in order to make the loan beneficial for them.

Example

Think about it like this. You want to bake a cake for your best friend's birthday, but you don't have the ingredients. You ask your mum if she doesn't mind lending you what is required so you can bake the perfect cake. But there's a catch: not only do you have to give her back the ingredients you borrowed, but in addition to this, for the privilege of using them when you didn't have your own, you have to give her a slice of cake each week for the next four weeks.

> **Remember, the bank is not your friend and often loan agreements will not be in your favour. Also, you can't just give your bank manager cake like you would your mum!**

Credit union

What is it? Credit unions are non-profit financial organisations set up by members with something in common, such as living in the same area or working in the same industry.

What do you need to know? Credit unions seek to create a mutually beneficial financial community that helps those who aren't in a position to access traditional bank products. Not only do they offer products such as savings accounts with preferential interest rates, they are often willing to offer shorter term loans suited to your particular needs.

However, Credit unions generally won't allow you to borrow money that you won't be in a position to pay back. In most cases, you will need to be a member first and there's often a requirement that you actually build up your savings with them first.

Compound interest

What is it? Compound interest is built up when you earn interest on the money you've saved, and also on the interest you earn from it. Compound interest occurs when, instead of withdrawing money from the account, you let it 'compound' by allowing it to grow.

What do you need to know? By not withdrawing the money, you are allowing all previously earned interest to remain in your account so the sum from which you calculate interest becomes larger over time. Basically, interest on interest.

The concept of compound interest is probably one of the most important financial lessons that I've learnt. Leaving your money to grow may seem like the most basic words of wisdom to impart to you, but I really wish someone had taken the time to break it all the way down with me. Seeing the figures in black and white may have helped influence the financial choices I made.

Example

Your parents give you £1,000 to deposit into an account as a reward for your GCSEs. Let's say you earn 3% interest on that money.

In year one, you would earn an additional £30.

In year two, you would continue to earn 3% on the amount in your account. As your current balance would be £1,030 after year one, the interest earnt in year two would amount to £30.90 – leaving you with a balance of £1,060.90.

So, in year three, you would have £1092.73.

But, what if you left that money untouched for years and years? Or what if, in addition to the initial £1,000, you contributed £100 religiously each and every month for twenty years without withdrawing a penny? Well, I'll tell you, honey. It's definitely a lot of money. £34,572.17 to be precise!

Individual Savings Account (ISA)

What is it? An ISA is a savings account that is exempt from tax and offers tax-free interest payments on the balance in your account.

What do you need to know? There are several different types of ISAs:

• **Cash ISA**: This is your bog-standard individual savings account and the most popular ISA on the market

• **Stocks and Shares ISA**: This type of ISA is for those who wish to invest and are able to save their money long term in high risk and volatile stocks.

• **Innovative Finance ISAs**: These types of ISAs are high risk as using one involves you lending your money in return for a high interest rate, but there is no guarantee that the borrower will be in a position to pay you back – this could lead to you losing your initial investment.

• **Help to buy ISAs**: These were designed to help first-time buyers get on the property ladder, with the government providing 25 per cent boost to whatever you have saved.

• **Lifetime ISA**: This gives you a government bonus of 25 per cent of the money you put in; however, the money can only be used for your first home, or accessed when you are due to retire.

• **Junior ISA**: This is a way for children to get in on the action and build up their savings – however, no one has access to that account until the account holder has turned eighteen.

Rotating savings

What is it? If you are familiar with the terms 'pardna', 'susu', 'box hand', 'ekub', 'njangi', 'tanda', 'meeting, 'hagbad' or ayuuto', then you already have an idea of what rotating savings are. Described as community cultural saving schemes, they are non-regulated methods of saving where a group of people deposit regular sums of money over a fixed time period to someone chosen as the 'banker' in order to receive their 'hand' or payment instalment.

During the 1950s and 1960s, West Indian immigrant families prolifically resorted to using the pardna - a popular method of saving back home - in order to combat exclusion from traditional loan and banking options. Known as 'redlining', they often faced difficulties when seeking loans, mortgages or credit services in order to set up home simply because of their race. So, they often worked together as a community to pool money for purchasing their own homes - ensuring that a large number of the Windrush generation were able to become homeowners, against all odds.

These schemes require a lot of trust and integrity of character - and that includes not only the banker, but also your fellow members, who must be committed to paying in even after they have the pleasure of receiving their hand.

Example

Ten 'partners' agree to pay £10 each week for 10 weeks. Each member contributes the same amount at each meeting, and at the end of each weekly period one member takes the whole sum. In this case, that would be £100. The 'rotation' comes about as they start the process again until all ten members have received £100. For the system to work, the number of partners must be the same as the number of weeks the scheme lasts.

Vex money

What is it? Now, vex money isn't something you will learn about in any formal financial literacy class. It's not even something a finance guru is likely to tell you about. But, if you don't take anything else on board in this chapter, please remember this: don't walk on road without your vex money.

You may have heard your mum or aunties discussing it – you know those big people conversations you shouldn't be listening to? But 'vex money' is a Jamaican term for the additional emergency funds you take out with you, usually on a date or when you're in an unfamiliar environment. The idea is that if the person you're with vexes you, or makes you feel uncomfortable in any way, then you have enough money to leave. **On your own terms.** Whether you use the money to pay for your travel home, or pay the cost of your meal. Vex money gives you options. It ensures you have the ability to make the right decision for you without having to make any compromises.

Keep your money safe

A final point that I want to discuss is bank fraud. This is not a joke. **Do not share** your PIN, passcode, password or access to your bank account with ANYONE. Not even to someone claiming to be from their bank or the police.

I remember in Year 7, our school invited bankers to come to the school and help us set up our first bank account. All of my friends got one and we IMMEDIATELY shared our PIN codes with one another. Well, I didn't, I gave a fake PIN because my mum had already explained financial security to me in our home tutoring (lol).

Now, I'm not mentioning no names, but three of the girls fell out. Really badly. To the point they were cussing each other. Physically fighting. Even exposing each other's business.

To make matters worse, one of the girls stole the other girl's bank card from her purse during PE. Now, we obviously didn't know this at the time, so we all helped our friend look, but it was GONE. So, what happened next? The teef actually used the card and drew out all of her money. But how did she do it? Remember when I said that everyone was sharing their PIN code like it was a packet of crisps at break? My girl memorised the PIN and went straight to her nearest ATM!

But don't worry, the story doesn't end there. She got caught on CCTV. The fool didn't realise that she had committed a criminal offence. She truly thought she was just getting her own back. The finesser got finessed.

Police were called. Conversations were had. Luckily for her, they didn't press charges. But she did have to wear a school uniform on non-uniform day and she was grounded for life. I'm not really sure what's worse! KIDDING! You can definitely get in a lot of trouble and she was just lucky that her parents were able to fix the situation. Not everyone would be so lucky.

But remember, not every situation may involve someone you actually know. There may even come a time where you are **approached** by someone who wants to use your bank details to 'hold' some money. They may even offer you a cut for your help. Easy money, right? No, sis. Bank fraud is a serious criminal offence that could damage your financial future. Mobile phone contract? Mortgage for your dream home? Loan for the fanciest car? Dream job? Those opportunities can **vanish** if you are convicted of fraud – not to mention the potential jail time.

Yes, it may seem tempting. Criminals know this – hence why they specifically target and groom young people and students, exploiting those who are on low incomes and may need the extra money. But, when you cannot confirm exactly where the money in your bank account comes from, you could 'unknowingly' be laundering the proceeds of a crime, whether that be money made from trafficking, drugs or terrorism. Now, is that worth risking a conviction, a ruined credit history and the ability to live your best life on your terms?

Handling your business

Let's keep it real: not all of you will be in a position at this point to follow these tips. Having savings is not only a privilege, it's a **luxury** that not everyone can afford. You cannot save or budget your way out of poverty. You can't manage your money if there is no money to manage. It's impossible. How do you budget when there's no money, honey?

There is such a pressure to have the latest trainers and phone that sometimes it can feel like 'drip or drown' isn't just a phrase – it's a consequence of not being able to engage in the same things as everyone around you. If we don't have the necessary cash to hand, many of us will use 'buy now, pay later' schemes to gives us what we want when we want. Often, utilising methods that require you pay back high amounts of interest seem ridiculous on paper. Who wants to pay £75 extra for an item just because they don't have the full amount spare? But with many people living from pay cheque to pay cheque, it really isn't realistic to think that there won't be times where you will need to **borrow money to** make a purchase.

Ultimately, many people **fear** loans and borrowing money, but it's not necessarily a bad thing if you have a real understanding of what you're signing up for. Learning financial terms and having a real understanding of how banking institutions work and what the different options and products available to you are, is a major key in becoming grown and handling your business. So, take everything you have learned with a pinch of salt, and adapt it for your own situation to **prepare yourself for the future.**

Save save save

Alexandra Sheppard,
author and social media strategist

If I could give my younger self any advice – as well as 'don't text that boy back' and 'give the red hair dye a miss' – it would be this: it's never too early to start saving. The longer you have to save, the easier it is to reach your savings goal.

Say you want to have £1000 saved by your 21st birthday. If you're fourteen, you would need to set aside £2.75 per week to reach that goal. If you're seventeen, you would need to save £4.80 every week. And if you start saving at the age of twenty? You'd need to sock away £19.23 every week.

They key is to set aside what you can afford and be consistent. After that, all you need to do is plan how you're going to spend that hard-saved cash.

'I've learned that, yes, wealth is a tool that gives you choices – but it can't compensate for a life not fully lived, and it certainly can't create a sense of peace within you.'
Oprah Winfrey [5]

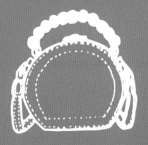

For us, by us

A love letter to Peng Black girls

By Melissa

This chapter is dedicated to all the girls that came before us. **The girls like you who will come after us.** And all the babygirls that are trying their hardest to find their purpose in a world that tries to tell them that they are too much whilst simultaneously showing them that they are not enough.

'I'm rooting for everyone Black.'
Issa Rae [1]

This may be the last chapter in this book, but really **it's the beginning of you becoming grown.** It's a celebration of everything that's brought you to this point. **Grown is an ode to Black British girlhood.** It's a documentation of the Black women and girls who continue to inspire and astound us. Not just those who were the 'first' to do 'it' or who paved the way by breaking down barriers - but those in our community who continue to do the work. Women who support us even when that support isn't always returned. Women who made a way out of no way.

When we say we are celebrating Black women, we mean **all** Black women. Not just the ones who look good, are speaky spokey or listened to their parents and faced their books. For too long, the Black women and girls who do the work and take the risks are pushed aside to allow for someone with a more palatable presence to take centre stage.

If *Grown* has taught you anything, I hope it is that mine and Natalie's mission is to create spaces where Black girls can come together to do what we do **unapologetically.** When we say that we do this ting 'for us, by us', we mean it. Whenever we link up, the first thing on our minds is ensuring that what we do and how we do it is for the benefit of **all of us.** If it is going to exclude or isolate even just one of our sisters, then it's not happening. Period. **What's the point in having a seat at the table if your sisters can't join you?**

Before *Grown* had a title or was even written, I just knew that I needed to create something that spoke directly to the unique experiences of Black British girls. Something that documented who *we* are and what *we* go through. **I wanted to speak about us in a way that only we understand.** I didn't want to code-switch. I didn't want to have to break anything down. For once, I didn't want to have to explain what anything meant. **Every word was written for you.** Every mention. Every quote. Every reference. Every recommendation is from a Black woman or girl. **Check the receipts!** Black girls are the focus and the feature of this book, and we did that with purpose and intention. You are enough and when you read *Grown*, I want you to remember that.

> *'I learned from my mother that if you have a chance to speak, you should speak. If you have an opinion, you should make it be known.'*
> **Ursula Burns** [2]

Black people make up 3% of the British population, and our impact and innovation is literally sewn into the fabric of this country. Black Britons and, specifically, Black British women have consistently paved the way. The Windrush Generation rebuilt this country brick by brick – with their contributions to public transport and the National Health Service – completely transforming Britain after the war. Today, the Black British creative renaissance is making waves in the arts, literature, media and music with our sound, style and spirit. Black people continue to provide a blueprint for everything that's cool and popping. **There might be no Black in the Union Jack, but the influence and impact that Black British people have had on this country is unrivalled.**

Claudia Jones responded to the Notting Hill race riots by organising a televised celebration of West Indian culture and heritage in St. Pancras Town Hall in 1965.

Today, Notting Hill Carnival is one of the largest street carnivals and recognised as the biggest celebration of West Indian culture in the UK. Now, we have platforms such as Black Girls' Book Club, Black Ballad, Black Blossoms and Black Girl Fest – all of which host events, exhibitions and festivals that allow us to come together, celebrate Black British culture and amplify the voices of Black women and girls.

Rt Hon. Diane Abbott MP became the UK's first Black female MP in 1987.

Since then, sixteen Black and mixed-Black women have taken office. Of course, it's not enough. But when Aunty Diane took the first steps and let it be known that Black women can and should take up space, she cleared the path so that over thirty years later women like community advisor Jen Davis can continue to create opportunities for Black women to get into politics. Jen's podcast The Consensus features Black and mixed-Black British women from across the political spectrum discussing politics and current affairs that matter to Black women and girls, ensuring our wants and needs are at the forefront of the discussion.

Margaret Busby became the UK's youngest and first Black female publisher in 1969.

Not only did Margaret revolutionise British literature as we know it, but she also created a path that made it possible for Natalie and me to be here writing this book. Because of Margaret we have **Sharmaine Lovegrove** at Dialogue Books; **Valerie Brandes** at Jacaranda Books; **Hena J. Bryan** at Bryan House Publishing, and **Aimee Felone** at Knights Of. These women are the founders of publishing house that seek to ensure that our stories are heard.

And let's not forget Amy Ashwood Garvey, who formed the earliest organisation for Black women in the UK with a mission to establish 'spiritual, cultural, social, and political advancement'.

Without Amy there would be no Black Girls' Book Club, Black Girls Camping Trip, Black Girls Knit Club, Black Gals Livin', Black Girls Hike, Black Girls Bookshelf, Black Girl Gamers, Bald Black Girls, Black Femme Film, Milk & Honey, ADHD Babes and so many more. Because of what Amy did, we know can carve out spaces that cater to us specifically. Whatever you are into. Whatever you like. There are other Black girls just like you who are waiting for you to just turn up and gist with them.

We speak about those who came before us to honour them for paving the way and showing us that nothing is impossible. **These women worked tirelessly to provide the foundation on which we now stand.** If you ever feel like things are becoming impossible and you don't know what steps to take next

'Stand up straight and realize who you are. That you tower over your circumstances. You are a child of God. Stand up straight.'
Maya Angelou [3]

or perhaps you feel alone and that no-one else 'gets it'. Remember, we have all been in our feelings at different stages of our life for countless reasons. Many of us have struggled to figure out who we are or what we want to do - but, as we always say, 'Tek time'. Life is a journey and not a race, and you aren't in competition with anyone but yourself.

It's hard to figure out how to do 'you' in a world that doesn't seem to make space for the person you are becoming. So, I've curated a list of women who inspired me to live my truth and believe in myself. Women who have shown me the meaning of sisterhood, loyalty, creativity and dedication. I wanted to recognise women who have inspired and revolutionised the way in which we view ourselves. Women who allowed us to ask for more. **Women who allowed us to dream. Women who *claimed* their rightful place by *taking* up space so that one day we wouldn't need to.**

Whether it's through the arts, academia, culture or tech, each and every person listed below has worked hard to create spaces, platforms and movements that have inspired us. You may have heard of some them before. They could have three or even three-hundred thousand followers on social media. Or perhaps they are under your radar. But one thing they all have in common is the way in which each and every one of them have uplifted Black women and girls.

'I said what I said.'
NeNe Leakes [4]

Lady Phyll Opoku-Gyimah AKA Lady Phyll, British political activist and Co-founder of UK Black Pride

Kuchenga Shenje, writer and journalist and a self-described 'avid reader of Black women's literature as a matter of survival' who has been featured in *Harper's Bazaar*, British *Vogue* and Netflix

Gena-mour Barrett, writer, journalist, recipient of the Roxane Gay Fellowship for Women of Colour Writing Fiction and one of Forbes 30 Under 30 for Media and Marketing

Margaret Casely-Hayford CBE, Lawyer and the first Black woman to become a partner in a city law firm

Toni-Blaze Ibekwe, editor-in-chief of British style publication *Wonderland* magazine

Christina Okorocha, **Ruby Jade-Aryiku and Rumbi Mupindu,** founders of Vamp PR – the first agency in the UK to solely focus on representing and developing Black digital talent

Malorie Blackman, author of the *Noughts and Crosses* series and former Children's Laureate

Shomi Williams, therapist, mental health advocate and founder of Lafiya Health – a platform established to raise awareness about issues surrounding mental and physical health in African and Caribbean communities

Lavinya Stennett, educational activist, historian and founder of The Black Curriculum – a social enterprise founded to address the lack of Black British history tight in schools

Bukky Bakray, actress and the youngest recipient of the BAFTA Rising Star Award

Kanya King MBE, CEO and founder of the MOBO Awards – an annual award show dedicated to the 'achievements in music of Black origin'

Rose Frimpong and **Nana Duncan**, host of Two Twos Podcast - an essential platform for the Black LGBTQIA+ community in the UK that centres the queer experience

Nadine White, Journalist and the UK's first and only race correspondent

Amina Patrice Bogle-Barriteau aka **Mina Lioness**, Grammy Accredited singer/songwriter and originator of the signature line, 'I did a DNA test and found out I'm 100% that b****'

Dorcas Magbadelo, founder of Dorcas Creates, product designer and illustrator of *Grown: The Black Girls' Guide to Glowing Up*

These women show us that **being YOU unapologetically is your secret weapon and your greatest gift.** All your experiences, challenges and life shaping moments is what being grown is about. So, if you ever feel like you are alone or there are things you are experiencing that you can't even explain and you need to **gas yourself up**, remember not to worry about whether you're enough or too much. Because you are on your way to becoming a grown Black girl – and that means **you are everything.** Period.

Or, if all else fails, I'll leave you with the words of my favourite philosopher, **Grace Latoya Hamilton**: 'Yuh cyaa beat me dat ah number one.'[5]

*I'm destined for GREAT things.
I stay READY.
I'm OWNING the person
I am becoming.
I'm WORKING towards
my goals.
I will NEVER let ANYONE
dull my shine.
I'm GROWN. PERIOD.*

Acknowledgements

First things first, we need to take a moment to say thank you to the women who attended the very first Black Girls' Book Club event. We tweeted, 'Who wants to attend a book club for Black women?' and without knowing who we were or what we were about, these women came through. What was originally just a moment between two friends became a movement.

Gloria Aboagye, Cecilia Aboagye-Mensah, Caroline Griffiths, Rumbi Rushambwa, Louise Kibirige, Flavia Toco, India Hosten-Hughes, Jahmila Lewis, Lizzy Macauley, Esmé Ara'Resa, Sarah Moreno, Imisoluwa Johnson-Epega, Abeke Popoola, Motunrayo Fagbayi, Rebecca Ferdinand, Tilly Ajala-Osinuga, Alexandra Sheppard, Tanya Dennis, Damola Odusolu, Sarah Lasoye, Joelyn Rolston Esdelle, Helen Aminashaun, Moyo Fujamade, Margaret Babatunde, Shanice Dover, Karis Morris-Brown, Frances Fadipe, Laura Wilson, Elisabeth Fapuro, Theresa Awolesi, Liz Coker, Sareeta Domingo, Victoria Adukwei Bulley, Joanne Munis, Rukayat Odusola, Samantha Williams, Elizabeth Fadeyi, Jeniz White, Annie Gibbs, Charn Williams, Susanna Ajayi, Zainab Conteh, Kitan Ososami, Chiamaka Echeta, Margaretha Bonsu, Vanessa Okojie, Wunmi Koik, Jennifer Davis and Krupal Patel.

Melissa

I feel like I already utilised every single bit of my word count to hail up and acknowledge those who made all of this possible, but I really do want to say a special thank you to those who have supported me on this journey.

Can I break the rules and acknowledge my younger self first?! Anyways, chile. Love to baby Melissa. Eleven-year-old me spent her summer holidays attempting to bribe the staff at Ordnance Road Library to be allowed to take out more than six books would be living for this moment. You really manifested everything you ever wanted. Remember this always: you are the woman you dreamt of becoming.

HCQ, you know what it is. Thank you for ensuring that all my dreams become a reality. I love you for real.

Mummy, Charles Lowe and Yasmin – because of you I believe I can do anything. Thank you for always seeing the best in me.

Thank you to Lauren 'my spirit took to her' Gardener. Not only an incredible agent, but a great friend and the true definition of 'ride or die'.

A big thank you to the entire team at Bloomsbury – especially Aunty Sharon, Isobel, Katie, Bea, Emily, Mattea and Jade – for giving us the space to create a body of work that truly centres the experiences of Black British girls and those have that lived it.

Thank you to my darlings Dorcas Magbadelo, Leah Jacobs-Gordon and babygirl Meena Alexander. Having a team of Black women shape Grown from inception to publication has not only been life-changing but also life-affirming. We really did this. Grown is for all of us.

Love always to my BGBC darlings, Benz Punani Book Readers and Authoresses. Without your love and support, none of this would have happened. Did y'all read the book?

Thank you to Aunty June Sarpong. With your full glossy lips, charisma and charm, you showed a generation of Black girls that the world was ours and everyone else was just living in it.

Finally, to anyone who has ever been told you are too much – don't pay attention to those who have yet to realise that they are more than enough.

Natalie

Firstly, I want to thank God. Never did I think I would be publishing a book, let alone a love letter to my younger self and the young Black beautiful girls growing up. Thank you for giving me such a privilege.

To Patrice, Pauline and Isaac Jnr. Thank you for being so supportive of me, looking after me and caring for me. Everything I have I owe to you, and I hope I have made you proud. To Aunty Dawn and Jasmine – thank you for always feeding me and encouraging me to be nicer to myself. I really love and appreciate you. To my Huddersfield Famalabams and The Carters – thank you for being such a lovely supportive family.

To my tribe, my soul circle – Caroline, Cherene, Krupal, Kristina, Chimme, Angel, Lianne, Lydie, Kemi – thank you for always listening and supporting me. You are all worth your weight in gold. Your sisterhood is priceless.

To all the beautiful Black women I call friends – I don't have the word count to name you all. To all BGBC members, the Authoresses and anyone who has blessed us with your presence at a BGBC Black Girls' Magic Brunch, A Seat at the Table, Dope Discussions, The Salon, In Conversations With … thank you for riding with us and for us. To every author who made time in their schedules to spend time with us, guide and invest in us – June Sarpong, Afua Hirsch, Dorothy Koomson, Diana Evans, Sharmaine Lovegrove, Candice Carty-Williams and Angie Thomas, to name a few.

To the dopest agent to walk these streets, Lauren Gardner: thank you for believing in us and getting us here – I am so grateful to you for your support and care. To the darlings Meena Alexander, Dorcas Magbadelo and Leah Jacobs-Gordon – you worked so hard to make sure Grown was the best it could be. To the incredible team at Bloomsbury – Isobel, Sharon, Bea, Katie and everyone else – thank you for working so hard on Grown and giving it your love and care; I am so grateful to you.

Clint, you are an inspiration. Sam, thank you for reminding me to write every day and looking after me – I appreciate you dearly. Malachi, thank you for our walks – they got me through some very tough times.

To Mel, there isn't much I can say to express my thanks to you. You have been riding for me since day one and look where we are. Thank you.

And I want thank myself, for never giving up and continuing to work hard at everything you put your mind to. This is just the start mama.

With thanks to our contributors

Afua Hirsch

Alexandra Sheppard

Audrey Indome

Bolanle Tajudeen

Candice Carty-Williams

Chanté Joseph

Chelsea Kwakye

Claudine Adeyemi

RT Hon Diane Abbott MP

Dorothy Koomson

Dr Anne-Marie Imafidon

MBE Ebinehita Iyere

Emma Dabiri

Faridah àbíké-íyímídé

Fiona Timba

Georgina Lawton

Gina Knight

Hannah Lee

Ibi Meier-Oruitemeka

Jade Bentil

Jay-Ann Lopez

Trina Charles

Jamelia Donaldson

Joan Andrea Hutchinson

Jumoke Abdullahi

Kadian Pow

Kafayat Okanlawon

Karis Beaumont

Kasey Robinson

Kayela 'LaLa Love' Damaze

Kelechi Okafor

Kym Oliver

Lillian Alfred

Liv Little

Melanie Brown

Nyome Nicholas-Williams

Phoenix Brown

Rachael Corson

Raifa Rafiq

Ruby Williams

Sara Collins

Sareeta Domingo

Shakaila Forbes-Bell

Sharmadean Reid

Sharmaine Lovegrove

Sinai Fleary

Sorayah July

Tobi Olujinmi

Vanessa Sanyauke

Notes

1: Is that you, yeah?

1 Audre Lorde, 'Poetry Readings & Rap Sessions' workshop flyer, The New York Public Library, 1971.

2 Zadie Smith, *Changing My Mind: Occasional Essays*, Hamish Hamilton, London, 2009, *p 10*.

3 Zora Neale Hurston, *Their Eyes Were Watching God*, Virago Press, London, 2020, p.181.

4 Hurston, *Their Eyes Were Watching God, p.* 220.

5 Professor Kimberlé Crenshaw, 'Demarginalizing the Intersection of Race and Sex', University of Chicago Legal Forum, Vol. 1989, Issue 1, 1989, p.149.

6 Amandla Stenberg, Young, Gifted and Black award acceptance speech, BET Black Girls Rock! Awards, 2016.

7 Viola Davis, quoted in Karen Valby, '"The Help": All the Dish', Entertainment Weekly, 5 August 2011, https://ew.com/article/2011/08/05/help-all-dish/.

8 Audre Lorde, 'Learning from the 60s' (speech, Malcolm X weekend at Harvard University, Cambridge, Massachusetts, February 1982). Archived in BlackPast, 12 August 2012, https://www.blackpast.org/african-american-history/1982-audre-lorde-learning-60s/ .

9 Maya Angelou, Foreword in Patricia Hinds and Audrey Edwards, *Essence: 25 Years Celebrating Black Women*, Harry N. Abrams, Inc., New York, *1995, p 13*.

10 Gabriel Alvarez, 'Beyoncé: Mighty Fly', *Complex,* 19 July 2011, https://www.complex.com/music/2011/07/beyonce-2011-cover-story-gallery.

11 Jessica Bennett, 'Lizzo defends booty-baring look, calls Rihanna her "inspiration"', *Page Six,* 10 December 2019, https://pagesix.com/2019/12/10/lizzo-defends-booty-baring-look-calls-rihanna-her-inspiration/.

12 Tre'vell Anderson, 'Marsai Martin may be young, but she's pulling the biggest "black-ish" laughs', *Los Angeles Times,* 20 July 2017, https://www.latimes.com/entertainment/la-ca-black-women-comedy-marsai-martin-20170720-htmlstory.html.

13 tvARTUR, 'Mariah Carey about Beyonce and J.Lo', YouTube, 19 January 2008, https://www.youtube.com/watch?v=-lposG3n5u4.

14 Candace Hasan, '*Essence* Festival 2019: Ava DuVernay Wants to Change the Fact that "90% of Entertainment is Produced by White Men"', *Essence,* 6 July 2019, https://www.essence.com/awards-events/2019-essence-festival/ava-duvernay-black-women-film-essence-festival-2019/.

15 Hurston, *Their Eyes Were Watching God,* p.88.

16 Hadley Freeman, 'Unmasked singer: Kelis on music, men and her missing money', *The Guardian,* 30 January 2020, https://www.theguardian.com/music/2020/jan/30/unmasked-singer-kelis-on-music-men-and-her-missing-money.

2: I woke up like this

1 An interview with Beyoncé in *SHAPE*, April 2013.

2 Lupita Nyong'o, Best Breakthrough Performance Award acceptance speech, Essence Black Women in Hollywood Luncheon, 2014, https://www.youtube.com/watch?v=mrD7HGjghrE.

3 'Lupita Nyong'o on racism, colourism and Justin Trudeau', *BBC Newsnight,* 8 October 2019, TV. https://www.bbc.co.uk/programmes/p07qh3d8.

4 Niki McGloster, 'Gabrielle Union Covers EBONY Magazine, Discusses True Love and Self-Esteem', *Vibe,* 8 September 2012, https://www.vibe.com/2012/09/gabrielle-union-ebony-magazine-self-esteem-younger-self.

5 Jason Chandler, 'Chewing Gum's Michaela Coel Brings Biting Wit That Won't Lose its Flavor', *Vibe,* 3 April 2017, https://www.vibe.com/2017/04/next-michaela-coel-interview.

3: Crowning glory

1 Sasha Bronner, 'The 24 Best Things Said Backstage at the 2014 Oscars', *HuffPost* US, 3 March 2014, https://www.huffingtonpost.co.uk/entry/oscars-backstage_n_4888060?ri18n=true.

2 Gina Knight, interviewed by Emma de Clercq, https://www.infringe.com/gina-knight/.

3 Dr Afiya Mbilishaka , 'PsychoHairapy: Using Hair as an Entry Point into Black Women's Spiritual and Mental Health.' *Meridians: feminism, race, transnationalism,* Vol. 16, No. 2, 2018, pp. 382–392. muse.jhu.edu/article/696151.

4 Sylene 'SylJoe' Joseph, 'I Don't Always Love My Kinky, Coily Hair, but I'm Trying', *Zora,* 8 December 2019, https://zora.medium.com/an-honest-review-of-my-tightly-coiled-natural-hair-17e0dbc609a2.

5 Joan Andrea Hutchinson, 'Dat Bumpyhead Gal', from *Jamaica Ridim & Ryme,* 2010. CD.

6 Alice Newbold, 'Misa Hylton, Stylist To Lil' Kim & Mary J Blige, On Why Her Work Is Not "Urban"', UK *Vogue,* 23 June 2020, https://www.vogue.co.uk/fashion/article/misa-hylton-fashion-anti-racism.

7 Madam C. J. Walker, quotes in Roberts, Blain, *Pageants, Parlors and Pretty Women: Race and Beauty in the Twentieth-century South,* 1st edition, University of North Carolina Press, Chapel Hill, 2014, p.66.

4: Squad goals

1 'Q&A: In Zadie Smith's 'NW', Some Harsh Truths About Friendship', *PBS News Hour,* 31 October 2012, TV, https://www.pbs.org/newshour/arts/conversation-with-author-zadie-smith.

2 Alice Walker, attrib.

3 *Beyoncé: Life is But a Dream,* dir. Ed Burke, Beyoncé Knowles and Ilan Benatar, HBO, 2013.

4 Audre Lorde, 'New Year's Day' in *The Collected Poems of Audre Lorde,* W. W. Norton & Co. Inc., New York, 1997, p 71.

5 Nikki Giovanni, 'The December of My Springs' in *The Selected Poems of Nikki Giovanni*, William Morrow & Co., New York, 1996, p. 158.

6 Shirley Chisholm, quoted in 'This Day in History: Shirley Chisholm Became the First Black Woman Elected to Congress', Women You Should Know, 5 November 2014, http://womenyoushouldknow.net/day-history-shirley-chisholm-became-first-black-woman-elected-congress/.

7 Zora Neale Hurston, *Their Eyes Were Watching God*, Virago Press, London, 2020, p. 6.

8 'New Attitude, Same ATL' (Series 2, Episode 1), *The Real Housewives of Atlanta*, Bravo, 2009.

5: Reclaiming your time

1 Zora Neale Hurston, '*How It Feels to Be Colored Me*', *I Love Myself When I Am Laughing: A Zora Neale Hurston Reader*, The Feminist Press, New York, p. 250.

2 *Oxford English Dictionary*

3 *Ibid.*

4 Reni Eddo-Lodge, *Why I'm No Longer Talking to White People About Race*, Bloomsbury, London, 2017, p. 63.

5 Assata Shakur, 'July 4th Address', given 4 July 1973, published in Joy James (ed.), Imprisoned Intellectuals: America's Political Prisoners Write on Life, Liberation, and Rebellion, Rowman & Littlefield, Lanham, 2003, p. 119.

6 Naomi Osaka, interviewed on ESPNW, 9 September 2020.

7 Natasha, quoted in Aamna Mohdin and Lucy Campbell, 'Young, British and black: a generation rises', *The Guardian*, 29 July 2020, https://www.theguardian.com/uk-news/ng-interactive/2020/jul/29/young-british-black-voices-behind-uk-anti-racism-protests-george-floyd#3.

8 Dr Moya Bailey, 'More on the origin of Misogynoir', moyazb.tumblr.com, 27 April 2014, https://moyazb.tumblr.com/post/84048113369/more-on-the-origin-of-misogynoir.

9 Toni Morrison, 'What the Black Woman Thinks About Women's Lib', *The New York Times,* New York, 22 August 1971, https://www.nytimes.com/1971/08/22/archives/what-the-black-woman-thinks-about-womens-lib-the-black-woman-and.html

10 Shirley Chisholm, quoted in 'This Day in History: Shirley Chisholm Became the First Black Woman Elected to Congress', Women You Should Know, 5 November 2014, https://womenyoushouldknow.net/day-history-shirley-chisholm-became-first-black-woman-elected-congress/

11 Labinot Kunushevci, 'The Representation of African-American Women: An Interview with Patricia Hill Collins', *Global Dialogue: Magazine of the International Sociological Association,* Vol. 7, Issue 1, March 2017, https://globaldialogue.isa-sociology.org/the-representation-of-african-american-women-an-interview-with-patricia-hill-collins/.

12 Bonni Angelo and Toni Morrison, 'Toni Morrison: The Pain of Being Black', *Time,* 22 May 1989, http://content.time.com/time/subscriber/article/0,33009,957724,00.html.

13 Nicole Dennis-Benn, 'A Woman-Child in Jamaica', *The New York Times*, New York, 30 July 2016, https://www.nytimes.com/2016/07/31/opinion/sunday/a-woman-child-in-jamaica.html.

14 Monique W. Morris, *Pushout: The Criminalization of Black Girls in Schools*, The New Press, New York and London, 2016, p. 33

15 Fannie Barrier Williams, 'The Colored Girl', first published in *The Voice of the Negro,* June 1905, pp.400–403. *Collected in The New Woman of Color: The Collected Writings of Fannie Barrier Williams,* 1893–1918 (ed. Mary Jo Deegan), Northern Illinois University Press, 2002, p.400-403.

16 Shirley Chisholm, quoted in 'This Day in History: Shirley Chisholm Became the First Black Woman Elected to Congress', Women You Should Know, 5 November 2014, https://womenyoushouldknow.net/day-history-shirley-chisholm-became-first-black-woman-elected-congress/

17 Zora Neale Hurston, '*How It Feels to Be Colored Me', I Love Myself When I Am Laughing: A Zora Neale Hurston Reader*, The Feminist Press, New York, p. 250

7: Yours faithfully

1 Janelle Monáe, @JanelleMonae, 20 July 2012, Tweet, https://twitter.com/janellemonae/status/226371873347338240?lang=en.

2 Lauren London, interviewed in 'Lauren London: The Girl You Love, The Woman You Should Respect', *Rolling Out,* 20 April 2011, https://rollingout.com/2011/04/20/lauren-london-the-girl-you-love-the-woman-you-should-respect/.

3 Zora Neale Hurston, *Dust Tracks on a Road,* J. B. Lippincott & Co., Philadelphia, 1942, p. 169

•Jacqueline Woodson, *Hush*, Penguin, New York, 2002, p. 91.

8: Got skills

1 Marva Collins, *Ordinary Children, Extraordinary Teachers*, Hampton Roads Publishing Company, Newburyport, 1992, p. 114.

2 Ava DuVernay, SXSW Festival keynote speech, 14 March 2015.

3 Danielle Newnham, 'Interview with Serial Entrepreneur Sharmadean Reid', *Medium*, 22 August 2018, https://medium.com/founder-stories/interview-with-serial-entrepreneur-sharmadean-reid-63b42a4fe2d1.

4 Nick Duerden, 'Malorie Blackman: The Children's Laureate talks writer's block, Noel Gallagher and being a warlock', *The Independent,* 17 November 2013, https://www.independent.co.uk/arts-entertainment/books/features/malorie-blackman-children-s-laureate-talks-writer-s-block-noel-gallagher-and-being-warlock-8942592.html.

5 Lisa Nichols, interviewed by Rhonda Byrne, dir. Drew Heriot, The Secret, dir. Drew Heriot, Lisa Nichols and Rhonda Byrne, Nine Network, 2006.

9: Secure the Bag

1 Maya Angelou, interviewed by Oprah Winfrey, *SuperSoul Sunday*, 19 May 2013.

2 Toni Morrison, *Beloved*, Vintage, London, 1997, p. 273.

3 Lorraine Hansberry, *A Raisin in the Sun*, Random House, New York, 1959, Act III, p.63.

4 Issa Rae, Rising Star Award acceptance speech, BET. Presents the American Black Film Festival Honors, 17 February 2017.

10: Money moves

1 Barbara Jordon, quoted in Frank Daniels III, 'Barbara Jordan helped break barriers', *The Tennessean*, 21 February 2014, https://eu.tennessean.com/story/opinion/columnists/teachable-moments/2014/02/21/-barbara-jordan-helped-break-barriers-/5653117/.

2 Cardi B, interviewed in Rawiya Kameir, 'Cardi B Did It Her Way', *The Fader*, Issue 110, July/August 2017, https://www.thefader.com/2017/06/22/cardi-b-cover-story-interview.

3 Oprah Winfrey, 'What Oprah Knows for Sure About Money', *The Oprah Magazine*, March 2008, https://www.oprah.com/omagazine/what-oprah-knows-for-sure-about-money.

4 Cardi B, Instagram post 26 February 2018 [cardi.hennessy], quoted in India Pougher and Nerisha Penrose, 'Cardi B Wants You To Feel "Poppin" In Her Fashion Nova Collection', Elle, 29 October 2018, https://www.elle.com/fashion/a19755367/cardi-b-fashion-nova-collaboration/ ."

5 Oprah Winfrey, *The Path Made Clear: Discovering Your Life's Meaning and Purpose*, Flatiron Books, New York, 2019, p. 234.

For us, by us

1 Issa Rae, quoted in Erin Nyren, 'Issa Rae at the Emmys: 'I'm Rooting for Everybody Black', Variety, 17 September 2017, https://variety.com/2017/tv/news/issa-rae-at-the-emmys-im-rooting-for-everybody-black-1202561838/

2 Ursula Burns, quoted in Alex Katsomitros, 'Against the odds: Ursula Burns' extraordinary rise to the top', World Finance, 1 April 2019, https://www.worldfinance.com/markets/against-the-odds-ursula-burns-extraordinary-rise-to-the-top

3 Maya Angelou, quoted in Linda Wagner-Martin, Maya Angelou, Bloomsbury, London, 2021, p.131.

4 Nene Leakes, 'Renuion Part 3' (Series 6, Episode 25), The Real Housewives Of Atlanta, Bravo, 2014.

5 Grace Latoya Hamilton, 'Reunion' (Series 7, Episode 18), Love & Hip Hop Atlanta, Monami Entertainment Eastern TV, 2018.